THE VALUE OF
ROTTING PUMPKINS

The Art of Teaching Elementary School

COLLEEN N. THRAILKILL, ED.D.

ARCHWAY
PUBLISHING

Archway Publishing books may be ordered through booksellers or by contacting:

Archway Publishing
1663 Liberty Drive
Bloomington, IN 47403
www.archwaypublishing.com
844-669-3957

Interior Image Credit: Kathryn Mizuchi, Wayne Thrailkill, Pamela Brunschwyler

ISBN: 978-1-4808-9954-4 (sc)
ISBN: 978-1-4808-9952-0 (hc)
ISBN: 978-1-4808-9953-7 (e)

Library of Congress Control Number: 2020922629

Print information available on the last page.

Archway Publishing rev. date: 01/20/2021

To Wayne

CONTENTS

INTRODUCTION

When I retired from teaching elementary school in 2010, I began writing about my teaching years, mostly as a piece of family history to pass along to my children and grandchildren. Eventually, though, it grew into a story about a job I loved, and I realized it might also have value for student teachers, beginning teachers, and veteran teachers.

At its core, this is a story about growth. No teacher is the best she or he can be from the first day in the classroom. It's over time and with experience that we develop skill and knowledge and learn the art of teaching. This book will show you how I grew, from an almost clueless novice in 1974, to an experienced teacher with an advanced degree when I retired in 2010.

In this book you will discover a sure-fire way to teach fifth graders how to think in a different number base, and the technique for using a rotting pumpkin to teach second graders a sense of environmental responsibility. You'll find out how to make use of teachable moments, and you'll reflect on the techniques we teachers use to meet the needs of every learner in our classrooms.

The comprehensive collection of references will help you find helpful resources for yourself and extensive literature for your students, and the appendix contains detailed directions for many of the projects referred to in the text.

My hope is that this book about my own teaching journey will supply you with useful curricular ideas, a few laughs and thoughtful advice which will help you to be a better teacher yourself as you master the art.

Colleen Nugent Thrailkill
August, 2020

PREFACE

It would be a mistake to say I aspired to be a teacher from an early age. However, there were a few signs in my youth that teaching, or maybe librarianship, lay in my future. When I was in second grade, my best friend, Michelle Kay Doeden, was a first grader. We liked to play school together and I, the older second grader, would help her "learn to read." I can't remember exactly what it entailed, but one day, her teacher stopped me in the school hallway, and said she had heard I was teaching Michelle to read. I acknowledged that was true, and the teacher said, "Good work." I swelled with pride. A few years later, when I was nine years old, I established a lending library in the basement of my house. I loaned out my personal books to kids in the neighborhood, and fondly remember how much fun it was to make check-out cards for each book so I could keep track of my treasured books' circulations. Knowing me, though, I was probably pretty bossy about pestering my friends to get the books back to me in a timely way.

That was it for my teaching career for a long time. In high school I developed an interest in sociology and psychology, and took science fair projects to the state science fair in those subjects my junior and senior years. As an outgrowth of one of my science fair projects, I took a summer job at Camp Challenge, Florida's Easter Seal Camp for handicapped children. I was a camp counselor for a cabin of campers who had all kinds of disabilities such as cerebral palsy, Down's syndrome, and blindness. It was an interesting, fun-filled summer for which I received room and board and $100. I headed to Atlanta for college the fall of 1966, planning to major in sociology or psychology, with no clue at all of what I would do with the degree once I had it.

My future mother-in-law ran a day care center in Florida, so another summer job I held during college was working for her. On a few occasions she remarked that I would make a good teacher, but I, an only child, laughed at the idea I would ever want to teach a crowd of children.

My husband and I married in 1968, when I was a college sophomore. At the end of that year our oldest son, Michael, was born. My college classes at this point included Psychology of the Family, Study of Human Personality, Social Psychology, and Child Development, among others. Michael supplied me with endless opportunities for real life observation and extension of the psychology and sociology topics I was studying in school. I graduated from Emory University in June of 1970 with a Bachelor's degree in Sociology, and many assorted psychology classes under my belt. I spent the entire summer job hunting, with no luck. My one and only possibility came from an ad I had put in the newspaper (a not-uncommon mode of job hunting back in those days). A man called me one day and said he worked at the Georgia Mental Health Institute. He described in great detail research he was doing on fetishes, and asked if I would be willing to be a research assistant. I was so excited! He set up an appointment at the Mental Health Institute for a few days hence. When I turned up as scheduled, I was informed no such person worked at the hospital. I assume it was a hoax by some creepy guy who got his jollies by talking about his own fetishes. My job hunting in the field of sociology reached a new low with that experience.

Because I badly needed a job, I returned to work for a day care center where I'd been employed part-time during college. Sheltering Arms Association of Day Nurseries is a special place. It opens its arms to Atlanta's needy families, and provides a quality day-care, preschool, and safe after-school haven. I was hired as a full-time employee, filling in for absent teachers, driving the van that dropped off and picked up the after-school kids, and supervising the school aged children when they came in after the end of each school day. I learned a lot working at Sheltering Arms, maybe most importantly never to threaten to leave behind a recalcitrant five-year-old who refuses to get in the day care van. She might just be willing to let you leave her behind. (The lesson here, whether you're a teacher or a parent, is never threaten something on which you are not willing or able to follow through). About three months into this job, I realized I was really enjoying it, and I began to finally seriously think about what might be involved for me to become a teacher. A woman named Rita Tucker was an enormous inspiration and influence for me at this time in my life. Mrs. Tucker was the day care center's supervisor. She was a jolly, plump, gray-haired woman who treated every child who walked in the door as her own.

I decided to go back to college to work on a Master's degree in Early Childhood Education and entered Georgia State College (eventually Georgia State University) the next fall, in 1971. Now my courses were more focused and specialized, such as Methods of Research, Curriculum Theory, Analysis of Learning Theories and Psychology of Play. I loved college. I loved the rigor, the chance to interact with thinking people, and even the pressure to write papers to a deadline.

Soon after I returned to college my husband and I decided to add a second child to our family. In February of 1972 I got pregnant, a little bit earlier than I had planned, and, as my classes progressed, I calculated my baby's due date would be one day after the date I would finish my Master's work. Oh, well, I just hoped this child would follow in his elder brother's footsteps, and arrive a few days after the due date.

My last term at school was to be spent in a practicum, student teaching in an elementary school. Unfortunately, as my college counselor attempted to place me for the course, none of the local public schools was willing to take me in what would be an advanced state of pregnancy. I grew more and more discouraged as one school after another said, "No. We don't want an extremely pregnant student teacher." Finally, though, a contact who was a principal at The Galloway School, a local private school, agreed to let me do my internship there. I was placed in a second/third grade multiage class. My supervising teacher was Carole Noonan. She was knowledgeable in her field, wise, patient, and kind. In her multiage class, she taught her students, and me, to strive for maturity, to become independent and self-motivated learners, and to always be willing to help one another master a new skill.

Luckily for me, our second son, Patrick, arrived exactly on his due date, so I managed to complete all of my course work and earn my degree, a Masters in Early Childhood Education, at the end of 1972. Not long after this my husband and I and our two little boys moved back to Orlando, Florida, an area where both of us had grown up. We bought a house, settled in, and I enjoyed applying my early childhood studies to the raising of two little boys. After a while, though, I thought it might be a good idea to put in a teaching application with the Orange County School System. I went down to the county office and filled out the paperwork to become a kindergarten teacher. As I was leaving the county school system offices, I heard a familiar voice. I followed it to an office, peeked in, and saw one of my own favorite teachers. Raymond Aldridge, had been my middle school social studies teacher in seventh and eighth grades and was now Orange County School's personnel director. He remembered me and we had a good time catching up. A couple of months later he called me with a job offer, and my teaching career officially began, one that would lead me from kindergarten to first grade, second grade, third grade and onward into an advanced degree working in gifted education, spanning the next thirty-six years.

The Beginning Teacher

· ● · ●

If I could say just one thing to parents, it would be that
a child needs someone who believes in him no matter
what he does.

Alice Keliher

M r. Aldridge's call had informed me that a kindergarten teacher
at a school close to my home had left unexpectedly, and he
asked if I'd like to apply for her position. It was mid-school year, and
the teacher has gone AWOL. Perhaps it should have set off a warning
bell, but I recklessly said, "Sure, I'm interested." I got the job, teaching
kindergarten at Lancaster Elementary in Orlando, Florida.

So in January of 1974 I officially became a public school teacher. On
my first day, the kindergartners said, "You're not our teacher. Where's our
teacher? We want our teacher back." It seemed no one had bothered to tell
them their teacher was gone. Not a very auspicious start. I didn't blame
them for being upset, and eventually we worked it out and managed to get
along, despite the fact that I was confused and disoriented at beginning
my first teaching job in the middle of the school year.

My name, Thrailkill, has never been an easy one for children to
master but, usually, once they know it, it sticks in their heads. However,
there might still be one of my former students who is still calling me
"Mrs. Killfrail," just as she did for the entire time I taught her that year.

One day, a woman came to the door of my classroom and started to walk in. I didn't recognize her and refused her admittance.

She said, "Don't you know who I am?"

I said, "No."

She said, "I'm the county supervisor of Early Childhood Education." Oops. Another time a parent came in to share his job with the class. He was a police officer and my five-year-olds listened to him with rapt attention for about ten minutes; then they wanted to touch him. Mostly, they wanted to touch his gun. He was being mobbed by twenty-four little people, and I could tell by the look on his face he was scared to death, so I rescued him. He might have preferred an angry adult mob to being pawed to death by kindergartners.

About a month into this job I got my hair cut and went from being long haired to being short haired. The first kid comment I got was the following Monday, "Mrs. Thrailkill, you look *terrible*." You can always depend on a child to serve up an honest opinion.

My first year of teaching and a new haircut

At the end of the school year, I concluded that I wasn't yet ready to work full time. I applied for a leave of absence from the school system. At the end of a year, the system would offer me another position, but I would not have the choice of having my Lancaster position held for me. If I wanted to come back, I would have to take whatever was offered.

In 1975, after a year at home with my two boys, I was offered a kindergarten position at Spring Lake Elementary School, in Apopka, Florida. I accepted. My principal was the husband of my own fourth grade teacher, a good thing, but the commute was a fifty-minute drive, not through heavy traffic, just many miles of travel on a diagonal from one corner of Orange County to the other. Between paying for a babysitter for the boys and buying gas for the car, I probably just about broke even that year. Kindergarten at this time was only a half-day for students, so I had a morning group and an afternoon group, twenty-eight kids in the morning and twenty-nine in the afternoon. No teacher's assistant, just me and a large crowd of kids.

Among the fifty-seven young children for whom I was responsible that year, a little boy named Preston was my most memorable. The truth is, it was his mother who was most memorable. On the first day of school, she escorted Preston into my classroom. I showed him a place to sit, but; as his mother prepared to leave, Preston became teary. This sometimes happens when a little kid starts school. I assured Preston's mother he would soon be fine, but I could tell she was reluctant to leave him with me. He was sobbing and gulping, and I was edging her toward the door. Just as it looked like she would be out and I could help him settle, she turned back to him and said, "Preston, I'm leaving." Fresh sobbing and gulping on Preston's part.

Why did she say that? Did she want him to feel bad about her going? Maybe so, because she did it several more times before I worked her out the door. Poor Preston! By this time, he was inconsolable, not to mention very loud and about to set off sobbing among the other twenty-seven children in the room. Preston cried for three days. Fortunately, the room was large, and I soon gave him a seat removed from the action and told him to come on over and join us as soon as he wanted to. On the fourth day, he became part of the group, and was fine for the rest of the year. He made a major impression on me, though. Years later, when I was referred to a doctor whose first name was Preston, I made sure he wasn't "my" Preston, just in case he might break into uncontrollable sobbing once he saw me again.

This was the year I first made the acquaintance of the Letter People. These were large, child-sized inflatable characters, each one representing a capital letter of the alphabet, and dressed in an outfit or sporting a body part that would help children learn a letter sound. Mr. B, for instance, had a large letter *B* on his front and he was covered in beautiful buttons, while Mr. F had a capital *F* and funny feet. They were part of a kid-friendly curriculum which effectively used phonics to build letter and sound recognition. Unfortunately, they were also inclined to spring leaks and often needed to be patched. The teacher in the classroom next door to mine usually took them home to fix them when that happened. She was an unmarried woman, quite a bit older than I was, and she used to joke the only males who made it into her bathtub were the Letter Boys when she went looking for the source of their air leaks.

Another memorable part of that year was the faculty talent show we presented at the end of the school year to celebrate America's 1976 bicentennial. I did an energetic cancan dance onstage with another teacher, and we had great fun. Our middle-aged principal dressed as Fonzie from the TV show, *Happy Days*. The students loved it.

Open-Space Teaching
and Moving On

* * * * *

Of course we need children! Adults need children
in their lives to listen to and care for, to keep their
imagination fresh and their hearts young and to make
the future a reality for which they are willing to work.

Margaret Mead

After a year at Spring Lake, I realized I would have to get a job
closer to home. I looked for a half unit of kindergarten, instead
of a full-time position, as my own two children were in need of more
of my time and attention. I found just what I needed at Winegard
Elementary, just a few miles from home. In a half-day morning class, I
worked with a new friend, Peggy Leftakis. We were assigned to teach
fifty-plus kindergartners in a large, open room.

This was the era of the open-space classroom concept, whose
proponents claimed children would learn better if they were taught
in large, open spaces with no walls between the classes on each grade
level. The intent was that teachers would collaborate, and the children
would benefit from the strengths of all the teachers at their grade level.
While it worked well with the two classes and the large room Peggy
and I shared, it was not so successful in the rest of the school, where

three or four classes shared the same space we had. In those rooms, the result was a cacophony, with teachers trying to talk over the sound of one another's and their students' voices. The open spaces eventually were divided up by low bookshelves, but that couldn't help the noise. I was vastly relieved I wasn't called upon to teach under such difficult circumstances

Peggy went on to have further experiences with open-space classrooms. A few years after we taught together, she taught first grade in a large area with a flimsy portable wall separating her space and that of a second grade group. If the teacher in the neighboring area turned off her light, the lights went off in Peggy's space too. After a few years, Peggy volunteered to move to an old portable classroom with no sink or bathroom, just to escape that arrangement! This was before the days of wet wipes or glue sticks, so Peggy kept a big tub of soapy water in her classroom for rinsing fingers, and twice a day the entire class would make a trip to the restroom located a few portables away. There was no covered walkway leading to her room so, if a Florida downpour occurred, the class would miss art or music class. Florida's frequent afternoon showers could also play havoc with school dismissal time.

Back in the classroom we shared at Winegard Elementary, we had the Letter People reading program. Peggy and I worked together to help our students learn letters and their sounds with the same engaging inflatable characters I had met at Spring Lake Elementary.

Near the end of our school year together, Peggy's husband, John, who was a photographer, brought his camera into the classroom after school hours. John and Peggy grouped the Letter People to make a variety of three letter words, and created a slide show. For instance, Mr. B with his beautiful buttons stood next to Ms. A with her a-choo who stood next to Mr. T who had tall teeth. The students could sound out the letters we had been working on to discover the word, *bat*. When we showed the slide show to our students, they came up with an explanation for the words. They claimed the Letter People had come alive after school hours and had held a party in our classroom.

About midway through our year of teaching together, I discovered I was unexpectedly pregnant. A few months later, Peggy learned she was pregnant too. I finished the school year, but then stayed home the following two school years. It seems pregnancy was rampant in Winegard Elementary for some reason that year. Who knows, maybe we all wanted to take a break from the open-space classroom craziness!

I enjoyed staying home with my three sons over the next two years, volunteering in their classrooms and in other schools around the county, and getting certified to teach Lamaze childbirth classes to expectant parents. I taught Lamaze classes at Orlando Regional Medical Center for the next twelve years and thoroughly enjoyed the contrasts between teaching young children and young adults. My Lamaze nights were my "Mom's night out" and exposed me to many new experiences. But by the fall of 1979 I was ready to return to teaching children also, but still wanted to work half time. I scoured the system for schools that had an odd number of kindergarten units and would need a half day teacher in the mornings. I was hired to work at Tangelo Park Elementary. I moved all my personal teaching supplies, bulletin boards, and large numbers of my personal books into my assigned classroom. Preplanning was spent preparing my classroom, setting it up just the way I wanted, and getting to know my colleagues.

The school year started, but no students came to my room. It seemed not enough kindergartners had registered to fill a class in the half unit I was to teach. I offered to help the one other kindergarten teacher. "No, thanks," she politely responded. I asked the principal what I should do. Her advice was, "Wait. We might have more children show up to register for the class. If not, the county will transfer you after about five weeks."

So, I waited – in an empty room, all set up and ready to go. I created units of study, made fancy bulletin boards, and lurked in the library. Every once in a while, I asked other teachers if I could help them. "No, thanks," they said. It was frustrating and depressing.

The five-week mark came, and I was able to transfer to Shenandoah

Elementary. It meant repacking and moving a huge amount of personal supplies, and then I was placed in a classroom with another teacher who would be sharing her morning class of kindergartners with me. The school year was well underway, and it was many more weeks before the students who were assigned to me would come to view me as "their" teacher. My colleague in this room was Mary McCown, and no one could have been more welcoming under what must have been a difficult situation for her too.

I learned a lot from Mary, who had an irrepressible twinkle in her eye and a love of kindergartners that matched my own. Her best lesson for me: "When someone asks about doing something different from what you're doing, don't say "Why?" say, "Why not?" She planned field trips all over the county, exposing our students to everything from the experience of milking cows to regular attendance at the theater. It was Mary who taught me the value of a home visit to every student in my classroom, an unusual thing for a teacher to do, and something I did for many more years to come.

Although we did have reading and math curriculum guides to help us teach our kindergartners, we also had great freedom in deciding how to teach them the basics and how to enrich their lives through education. I was always searching for topics that would sneak up on my students and teach them something valuable before they realized it. Kindergartners are sponges when it comes to learning anything new, so my job was fun for both me and my students.

One thing we studied that year was airplanes. The school is not far from Orlando International Airport, and planes flew over our playground constantly. My oldest son, Michael, who was a sixth grader, was fascinated by airplanes, so I enlisted his help to teach my students about them. He drew large, labeled pictures of each of the main passenger jets we saw every day out on the playground, and my students enjoyed identifying them. Then Michael came to school one day as a guest speaker on the topic of airplanes. He was a big hit. Michael visited my students another time, several years later, when I was teaching third grade. By this time, Michael was an architecture student at the University of Miami. He showed my students what he was doing to work toward his degree, and everyone was impressed with what a talented artist he was, again.

What do You do in Kindergarten?

· · · · ·

All I really need to know I learned in kindergarten.

Robert Fulghum

Gene Bratek, who worked as a headmaster at a school in Charlotte, North Carolina, told me this story: "It was the first day of classes at Providence Day School. As I walked the halls at the end of the academic day, I saw a kindergarten student getting ready to go home. I asked him how his first day was. He put his hands on his hips and said with a serious look on his face, 'I've been waiting allll my life to come to this school.' Then he promptly walked out the door with a big smile on his face."

Children look forward to beginning school. They are eager to learn to read, to find out the secrets of numbers, to go to music and art and physical education classes, and to make new friends. When I was a child, I can remember my eagerness to be able to read the Sunday funny papers in the newspaper. Every Monday morning, my grandmother in Florida would mail her Sunday funnies to me in Montana.

My mother would read me those funnies when they arrived, but I would constantly ask her, "When will I learn to read by myself?"

She always answered, "You'll learn to read when you start school."

The first day of school arrived and I set out in new shoes and a new dress and a state of high excitement.

At the end of the day my mother asked me, "Was it a good day?"

"Not so good," I answered in disgust. "I didn't learn how to read and you said I would."

One of the earliest and most valuable lessons I learned as a teacher of kindergarten children was to recognize how much growth happens during the year from age five to age six. We are all amazed at the rapid development of babies as they go from having no control of their limbs to crawling, then standing, then walking, in the short span of a year. It's important to recognize this rapid development is still happening in their brains and bodies when they walk into their first school experience. A few months between the ages of my students could profoundly affect what I should expect of them. Parents were often eager for their children to start school as soon as they were eligible, but I could see that when a child would be on the young side of the group he or she started with, there could be a benefit to keeping the child home for an extra year. I called this "giving a child a gift of time." Then, when they did start school, they would be among the oldest mentally and physically and would have an edge that would last throughout their school career, instead of always being the youngest in the group. Making a decision like this is not necessarily right for every child and parents know their child best, but it is absolutely worth considering.

One of my favorite college classes had been The Psychology of Play. In this class we studied how important play was in helping young children to learn and to prepare for more formal education. One day we students took a field trip to the Yerkes Primate Institute near Atlanta. Our assignment was to observe monkeys, all day long, with particular attention to incidents which appeared to be play. Monkeys play – a lot. Young monkeys, in particular, interact in ways which can clearly be seen to be playful, chasing each other, chattering, and enjoying socializing with their peers. Human children do the same things, as a way of learning about the world around them, thereby developing curiosity and problem-solving abilities.

Since I had worked in the summer and during college in camps and day care centers and had young children myself, I saw first-hand the value of unstructured play, just as I could observe it with the monkeys. As a kindergarten teacher, I helped my students begin to learn to read and do math. I also made sure my five- and six-year-olds had chances to share, treat each other fairly, apologize when they did something to hurt someone else, and clean up their own messes. And, of course, I made sure there were opportunities to play and have fun. We read lots of good books, sang songs together, made messy, gooey or gluey art projects (and, of course, cleaned up after ourselves). We painted pictures and made homemade play dough. (See the Appendix for the recipe.) We had recess – unstructured play time outside – and we had learning centers in the classroom. Kindergarten teachers had been taught to plan such that learning and playing went hand in hand. We had a minimum of strict curriculum guidance and, I must confess, I thought that was a good thing.

But sometimes I planned an activity for the sole purpose of fun. Thus it was we decided to try to catch a leprechaun. Before St. Patrick's Day, we read stories that asserted it was good luck to catch one of these tricky elves. If you caught him, he would have to grant you a wish. The kids and I brought some boxes from home, and students designed and decorated their leprechaun "traps." Before we went home on March 16, we set the traps up around the classroom. I had a plan. After the students left for the day, I sprinkled gold glitter around the room. Yes, I was fortunate to have a very kind school custodian. I made the traps look as though they had been sprung, though there was nothing caught in them. I wrote a taunting message, ostensibly from the leprechaun, on the chalkboard. When the students came into class the next day and saw the traps changed, they were convinced the leprechaun had come and might still be hiding in the classroom. They took off, looking everywhere. I had prepared for this and busily "helped" them to look. After a bit, I shouted, "I caught him!!!" I held up a small paper sack, and gave it a little shake so the kids could hear something was inside.

The students clambered to open the bag, but I suggested we keep on looking and maybe someone else would catch one. I closed the bag tightly as they all watched, and set it on my desk. After another five or six minutes, we gathered on the rug to open the bag and collect our wish. A student was given the sack and slowly opened it to find.......a small piece of folded-up paper inside and nothing else. We unfolded the paper and on it was written "Ha! Ha! You can't catch me!" How did the leprechaun get out? We all heard him in there when I shook the bag. We examined the bag and found a small tear in a bottom corner. "He kicked his way out!" "He chewed through the paper!" "He tricked us!!!"

Of course, it was all a set-up by me (a prewritten note in the bag and a pre-torn hole in the corner and a little sleight-of-hand) but nobody ever questioned it. We had much spirited discussion about what could have happened, and how we could have made better traps. The kids were determined to keep on trying to catch that tricky elf, even after they went home that day. It was a lot of fun and absolutely the stuff of which a good day in kindergarten is made.

Half-Day Kindergarten to All- Day Kindergarten

• ◦ • ◦ •

There are only two lasting gifts we can give our children – One is roots, the other is wings.

Unknown

I taught at Shenandoah for two years, but then the school's enrollment dropped enough to cancel my half unit. By 1981 I was on the road again, looking for another half-day kindergarten class, and was fortunate to find one not far away at Conway Elementary. I was to work at Conway for the next sixteen years, over four grade levels, with many colleagues and administrators who inspired me as I got to know the school community and my students and their families.

Half-day kindergarten was a perfect arrangement for me and, I thought, for five-year-old children too. They were exposed to an academic setting, changing topics and activities every twenty to twenty-five minutes, learning how to get along with other children and interacting with adults other than their parents. If they were in the morning group they went home at midday, to lunch and a nap if they needed it and still had ample opportunity to play; or, if they were in the afternoon group, they had a long, leisurely morning at home and then came to school in the afternoon.

Most parents preferred to have their children in the morning session. I actually preferred the afternoon group. Those afternoon kids had the benefit of me learning my teaching mistakes in the morning and being able to immediately correct them by the afternoon.

However, in 1982 Orange County bowed to pressure from the ever-increasing numbers of working parents who could not arrange for half-day day care before or after the kindergarten day. In my county and many other school systems in America, a full day kindergarten program was adopted. All-day kindergarten became mandatory in the state of Florida that year, required before entrance into first grade. I was unhappy to see this come, and arranged a leave of absence so I could stay at home the first year and again be a full-time mother.

The following year, with my own three children all in school, I returned to Conway to teach kindergarten full-time. After a few months, a representative from the county office informed my grade level she would be meeting with us to hear our impressions of all-day kindergarten. We gathered with her after school. I was in attendance but not giving much input because I was new to the program, so I had plenty of opportunity to observe. I noticed every time a teacher said something negative about the all-day program, the representative listened with sympathy. Every time something positive was mentioned, she scribbled away, making notes. From my vantage point, it sounded as though the teachers had more negative than positive things to say.

Imagine how surprised we all were a couple of months later when her report was published! She concluded from her extensive visits around the county that all-day kindergarten was a rousing success. I couldn't help but wonder if every school she visited got the same enthusiasm from her in writing down positive comments, and nothing written down for the not-so-positive comments. I guess this was my first exposure to a disappointing sense of disconnect between the county office and the classroom teachers. It wasn't my last, though. Several years later when the school system moved to year-round schools, criticism from the rank and file was discouraged (or possibly ignored?) again.

I worked at Conway Elementary School until 1997, first teaching kindergarten, then moving into first grade and eventually also teaching second and third grades there. Two years after I began teaching first grade, my principal informed me he needed me to return to kindergarten. My own three children thought it was hilarious that Mom had to be sent back to kindergarten from first grade. After I returned to kindergarten, the parent of one of my former students relayed a story from one of her son's early days as a first grader. She said he told her he had noticed a child who had been in kindergarten with him was still in kindergarten this year. She explained sometimes people needed another year in a grade in order to learn everything they needed to know. She asked if he'd noticed anyone else who had stayed back in kindergarten. He thought a few moments and then said, "Just Mrs. Thrailkill."

Truth be told, every year I taught any grade, I learned a lot myself. People often ask me which grade was my favorite to teach during my career. I always felt the grade I was in at that moment was my favorite. I delighted thoroughly in getting exposed to each developmental stage children pass through, and enjoyed the unique behavior, physical maturation, distinctive sense of humor, and interesting quirks that went along with any particular age level.

As I had learned a few years earlier from Mary McCown, I continued to make a home visit to every student in my class. Most of these occurred on our first teacher work-day of the school year, which usually fell in October. By that time, I knew the kids and they knew me. Early in the year I let parents know I would be making a short social visit to their child to get to know her or him on their own turf. I wanted to meet brothers and sisters, see my students' favorite toys, and meet their pets if they had any. I made it clear to parents this would *not* be a parent/teacher conference. If necessary, I arranged the visit for after school or even in the evening.

These visits were invaluable in helping me to gain a sense of the dynamics from which my students came. I often discovered my kindergartners or first graders were the English translators for their parents. I saw living conditions that helped me understand why a child might be coming to school tired or hungry or sad or rebellious, and I also saw the many ways families nurtured and loved their children and maintained strong connections between home and school. My students were very happy I wanted to get to know them better and, with the visits, their parents connected with me and felt comfortable communicating within the school setting. Only once did a parent refuse me permission to make a home visit. She said she felt it was an invasion of her privacy. Overwhelmingly, families were proud and honored that the teacher was coming to their child's home and they welcomed me.

One year I visited a home where a non-English-speaking grandmother from Indonesia was caring for the children. A wonderful odor greeted me as I walked in, and I commented on how delicious the chicken smelled that the grandmother was cooking. She motioned me into a chair at the dining room table, and set before me a large plate of fried chicken and bread. I munched and munched as she watched me, making sure I ate every bit of the meal she had fixed especially for me, or maybe for the family. I worried afterward I'd been taking food from the mouths of the children, but there was no escaping that grandma and her determined hospitality.

At Conway, I soon discovered one of the best ways to interest children in reading and math and writing and social studies and science was through cooking. Our cooking projects often started with a piece of literature (reading) which led into a recipe that children copied (handwriting lesson) to put into a book that would go home (home-school communication). We made the recipe together (math and science) and then enjoyed eating it (development of a sense of community and social skills).

One of my favorites of many recipes was Stone Soup. There are several good retellings of this story and I've included three in the Reference section at the end of this book by authors Anne McGovern,

Tony Ross, and Marcia Brown. It's an old folktale, which has been retold in many cultures (social studies!). It tells how some weary travelers trick stingy townspeople into making a delicious soup. You can check the Appendix for the recipe we used. The soup begins with a large stone, one I supplied and had thoroughly scrubbed before class. In with the stone and some water, the story tells how the townspeople added beef, potatoes, carrots, onions, salt, and pepper. We reenacted the story in class with different students assigned to bring different vegetables. After a nice simmer through the morning, we tasted the soup and were amazed that one could make soup from a stone. Many a mother asked me how on earth I had convinced her child to eat beef vegetable soup. The trick was easy. I asked every child to try only a little of the soup in a small paper cup. I said they were welcome to come back for more, but each time gave them only a little. Everyone was willing to try the little bit and almost everyone came back for seconds, thirds, and fourths, until the soup pot was empty.

A few years later, when I was reading several versions of Stone Soup with third graders, I asked for some original soup recipes from the students. Here's a sample of what I got:

Dead Soup

1. 2 or 3 dead frogs
2. 1 or 2 dead rats
3. 10 or more dead bugs (variety)
4. 10 socks (stinky)

    Stir. Then add fire crackers (a lot). Light them before adding to the soup. Then add a lot of noodles.

I passed the recipes along to parents in a newsletter with a disclaimer that none of them had been kitchen tested.

My kindergarten classroom at Conway was carpeted over almost the entire room, only having a small bit of tile around the sink in the back. When we painted, I had to keep the kids in the sink area to avoid carpet stains. One day in the fall, I had a group of four or five children lined up on the tile floor painting nice orange/brown/yellow/red pictures. Someone asked me for more orange, and I pulled a container from the cupboard and filled it with orange paint. What I didn't know was the container had a hole in the bottom. As I lifted it to take to the last child in the row, bright orange paint dribbled out and poured over every child on the floor. The kids thought it was funny. I'm sure their mothers didn't.

One day Daniel, one of my kindergartners, had just gotten a new haircut, and proudly showed it off to everyone in the class. Later, while we were out at recess, Thomas poured sand on Daniel's head. Daniel came storming over to me to report, "Thomas just poured sand over me," he bellowed, "and this is my new head!"

One year in kindergarten, I had a little boy named Martin on my class list. The first day of school his father brought him into the classroom. Martin was not happy to be there and was very teary. His father was finding it hard to leave him, but I gently eased him out the door with assurances Martin would soon be just fine. Remember, I was experienced at this by now. I watched Martin's dad from the window as he walked slowly toward the front of the school. He got about halfway to the sidewalk, and suddenly turned back and came into my room. He said, "I can't stand it," went over to Martin, took him by the hand, and walked him out the door. The other students and I could only stare. The school day went on.

About an hour later, I happened to glance out the window, and saw a woman walking toward my room with Martin firmly in tow. She walked in, sat him down, looked at me, said, "He's staying" and took herself out the door and left the school. That was undoubtedly the strangest first day of school I ever experienced.

5

Classroom Management

· · • · ·

The best methods for herding cats
"Herding cats - An idiom denoting a futile attempt to control or organize a class of entities which are inherently uncontrollable — as in the difficulty of attempting to command a large number of **cats** into a group (**herd**)."

From Wikipedia

Every beginning teacher must develop a classroom management system that works for her or him. It doesn't always happen in a teacher's first year, and it can be frustrating and demoralizing to discover that twenty-five or so kindergartners or first graders don't rush to do your bidding from the first day of school. I always felt it was best for student teachers to do their internship time in the fall, soon after school began, so they could see how an experienced teacher got students settled in and developed classroom rules and routines. Later in the year, it looks effortless but it's not, not for anyone.

One thing I realized early on was I should seriously over plan for the first week of school. I created lesson plans for that week with far more activities than I thought my kindergartners could do. Then, if something didn't work well or we finished it faster than I expected, I had back-ups. The scariest kind of day for a teacher of young children is the helpless feeling of not knowing what to do next, with another hour left to go in the school day. Talk about trying to herd cats!

The first week of school is so important in setting a class up to run smoothly. I will tell you about several methods I incorporated myself, and that I heard about from other teacher friends. I made sure the first day was a very positive experience; that my students knew I was excited to see them and eager for our school year to begin. The classroom would be set up for business and bright and inviting. Nametags would be on desks when the children arrived, along with an easy independent activity to do – a simple jigsaw puzzle cut from a greeting card or a ball of homemade play dough. (See the recipe for this in the Appendix).

By the second day, we were ready to sit down together and develop the rules to help our classroom run well. I wanted the rules to be limited in number (4-5) and created by my students. They were eager to make suggestions: "Listen to the teacher," "Do all your work," "Be nice," "Don't fight." Somewhere along the way a child would always suggest a variation of what I considered our most important class rule – "Treat other people the way you want them to treat you." The other rules might vary from year to year and grade to grade, but treating people the way you would want to be treated really covered just about every possible human interaction we might be faced with over the course of our year together. We would brainstorm six or seven suggestions, then discuss and vote on them. The four or five we thought were most important would be our final list. (I would always make sure the Golden Rule was worked in there somewhere.) Our collection would be prominently posted on the wall of the classroom and shared with parents.

All teachers find learning activities in a classroom run most efficiently if they can develop a signal early in the year to show their students when they want their attention. I've known teachers to use a countdown, to sing a song, blink lights, employ a hand signal, clap a pattern, or ring a bell. One of the most effective ones I ever saw teachers use was this: when she or he wanted to get the class' attention, the teacher said in a very quiet voice, "Clap three times if you can hear my voice." The students who are tuned in to the teacher will make the claps that are loud enough so other kids realize what's going on and will then listen too.

My friend, Joanne McCarthy, who taught for many years in North Syracuse, New York, told me that when she needed to use this method to get everyone's attention she would physically move herself close to a student she knew was listening before she would say anything. Then she knew she could count on the child to follow her direction and help her get the attention of the other students, no matter how much noise was going on in the classroom. When I introduced my signal the very first day of the school year and taught my kids to respond to it, I could get their attention even if we were engaged in several less-than-silent learning centers or different activities.

For third graders and older students, I knew several teachers who held regular class meetings to address issues of classroom conflict or management. This gave students a chance to be a part of classroom governance and instilled in them a sense of being invested in the success of their learning experience.

I often assigned classroom seating or lined my students up by varied criteria, such as hair color, letters of their first or last names, colors they were wearing, months of their birthdays, all the things I could think of to make forming a line to walk from place to place more stimulating and interesting. I did this because I remembered how much I had always wanted to be first in line as a child, and how annoyed and bored I was by always sitting or lining up in alphabetical order.

Sometimes a problem with student misbehavior causes a teacher to sit the student in a desk removed from other students. This can be a useful strategy for a child who initiates conflict with other class members or who has trouble concentrating with others around, but it should never be a permanent arrangement. We want a child to choose to be a part of the class and any child needs to know what behavior will help achieve that and aspire to reach it.

By the time I was teaching second grade, I had a reliable method for helping us monitor classroom behavior. I made a pocket chart with a labeled pocket for each student in the class, alphabetized by first name. Every pocket held five Popsicle sticks with the student's name written on each one. On my desk was a container. If a student broke one of our rules, I gave a warning. If that didn't fix the problem, the student had to take a stick from his or her pocket and put it in the container on my desk. Each stick meant five minutes of sitting idly while we had free time at the end of the day or recess time outside.

On Thursday of each week, a folder went home with my students. Graded work was inside and written on the outside of the folder was a place for the number of sticks the student had lost that week or a star sticker if no sticks were lost, a place for me and their parents to make comments, and a place for the parent to sign. Signed folders were due back the next day and, if they arrived promptly, I paid with a sticker. This method helped to maintain strong lines of home-school communication and put responsibility for that communication in the hands of students and parents

Liking children is probably the most important aid to classroom discipline you will ever have at your disposal. Children quickly can read you, even very young ones, and they'll know if you are enjoying your job and your interactions with them. Bluntly put, if you don't like kids, you have no business in the classroom!

Additionally, the importance of parents as partners with you in their children's education can never be underestimated. Close parent communication was a great aid for me in helping children get help they needed, and it emphasized to parents my belief in the essential nature of their role in their child's education.

Teaching Reading

· · ● · ·

If you can read this, thank a teacher.

Harry S. Truman

There is no sense of power greater than the one a teacher feels when she or he teaches a child to read. There is no more satisfying feeling than watching a light go on in a child's face as he or she realizes that those once unintelligible little squiggles on the page have meaning.

We don't all come to reading with ease. Some children do. My oldest son sat on his potty chair with *Dr. Seuss' ABC Book*, and began to learn letters and their sounds, seemingly all by himself. Reading is not so easy for many kids, and his two younger brothers struggled to make sense of letter forms and sounds and the way they worked together to make words. I never found an explanation for why reading is hard for some children and easy for others, but I also never grew tired of trying to help children unlock the magic of words.

I recently read an article in the newspaper about the benefits of teaching reading through phonics instruction versus whole language instruction. The author came down solidly on the side of phonics instruction being the best. During my long career as a grade school teacher, I made use of both methods and came to believe neither one was the definitive method for making powerful readers of children.

Phonics instruction teaches letter recognition and letter-sound association. From there, the next step is linking letter sounds to decode words. For many children, this is the key that unlocks words and can lead to understanding their meanings.

Whole language reading instruction focuses on teaching reading by encouraging students to select their own reading material based upon their interests. This method emphasizes the use and recognition of words in everyday contexts, thereby teaching reading by using the print that surrounds a child in his or her own environment. By developing recognition of frequently used "sight words," a child builds a foundation that leads to stronger reading fluency,

Strict phonics instruction can teach a child to use sounds to make words, albeit not necessarily with meaning attached. Whole language instruction can offer a child a meaningful interaction with literature, though not necessarily provide the tools to make a child a self-motivated, independent reader. I have been required to teach monotonous, scripted "reading" lessons of phonetically and artificially devised "Dick and Jane" stories that neither my students nor I enjoyed, and I've been instructed to "do whole language" with little or no direction on how that should happen.

Neither method works all by itself. Thankfully, most teachers manage to figure out just what is required to lead a student to learn to read – solid instruction in letter recognition and sounds linked with interesting and grade-appropriate literature to read. Add to this lots and lots of exposure to the printed word in the learning environment such as classroom signs, frequent use of a dictionary, journal writing, and letter writing. Supplement this with an abundance of interesting reading material available in the classroom, and much encouragement to use it. Be aware, children come to reading from many different beginnings, and be ready to meet each one of them wherever he or she is. With the use of all of these tools, you can create a classroom of readers. It sounds a little bit like magic, and it feels like it too.

My years spent in primary grades led me to the belief that first grade is the most important school year for learning how to read.

This year is the one in which a teacher takes the foundations of letter recognition and letter-sound knowledge five- and six-year-old students learned in kindergarten, and begins to build with them to create the structure that helps give six- and seven-year-olds the tools to impart meaning to a collection of words. If we don't teach a child how to decode sounds and make them become words when he or she is a first grader, we have missed a vital opportunity. Reading is so important that I came to feel first grade teachers should be the highest paid among us, perhaps second only to middle school teachers; who I believe are truly heroic humans for their willingness to teach young teenagers!

Books for beginning readers should have a limited, controlled vocabulary. They should tell a simple, but engaging story with appealing illustrations that can give cues to help the developing reader gain a sense of the story. There are many excellent books that achieve this end, and three of my favorite authors for beginning books are Mercer Mayer (who illustrated the wordless books about a frog and a boy), Else Holmelund Minarik (books about Little Bear) and Arnold Lobel (books about Frog and Toad). The series of I Can Read! books, published by HarperCollins, are organized in color coded levels and will help teachers and parents find the appropriate level for a child.

Many years into my career, I was tasked with working each day with a small group of nonreaders. These were fifth graders who were falling through the cracks. A few were immigrants who were still learning English, and a few were kids who had changed schools too many times and/or had not had enough support from home. We used a scripted program that taught letter sounds, skills in sounding out words, comprehension and vocabulary in rigid, sequential lessons. Initially I balked at using it, but I soon realized this was what these children needed to help them catch up – a program that went back to the beginning and covered the basics of how to read in a series of efficient and effective steps. It was satisfying to watch these children gain in competency and come to believe in themselves. We also studied a little poetry in the group, and I introduced them to Robert Frost's poem "The Road Not Taken," which gave us a chance to talk about life's choices and some of the challenges they would soon be facing in middle school.

During the years when I was a classroom teacher, I read chapter books aloud to my students every day after lunch. I knew early on children could understand more than they had the ability to read independently, so I could choose books that were two to three years above my students' reading level knowing they were not above their comprehension level. I knew reading aloud to children builds vocabulary and background knowledge. I knew it stimulates imagination, stretches attention spans, and enriches a child's working language.

In 1979, Jim Trelease published a very useful book on this topic, *The Read-Aloud Handbook*. For the next three decades, he added other books on the topic of reading aloud to children, which remain excellent resources for both teachers and parents.

One year, I conducted an informal poll among the members of my third grade classroom. Of twenty-four children, only five said someone read to them regularly. When I asked how many class members would like to have someone reading aloud to them, only four said "no," and the remainder said "yes." To the question "Why do you like to be read to?" a few of the answers were, "Someone reading out loud can make things have expression that you can't do when you read in your head." "They can read harder books." "It's a nice time to feel relaxed, to draw, to rest."

I read aloud *The Little House in the Big Woods* by Laura Ingalls Wilder, and my students learned about the resourcefulness of American pioneers living in the wilderness of Wisconsin in the last half of the 1800s. I read *The Indian in the Cupboard* by Lynn Reid Banks, and we came to appreciate the survival skills of Native Americans. I read *Time for Andrew* by Mary Downing Hahn and *Charlotte's Web* by E.B. White, *The Wizard of Oz* by L. Frank Baum, *Hatchet* by Gary Paulsen, and *Holes* by Louis Sachar. We laughed at the Ramona books by Beverly Cleary, and at Sachar's *Sideways Stories from Wayside School*. My purpose was to inspire my students to choose to read wonderful books like these on their own—not because they had to—but because they wanted to. One year I read *Where the Red Fern Grows* by Wilson Rawls, a terribly sad but wonderfully told story. By the end of the book I was passing out tissues for all of us, including me. I decided that was a story I would leave children to read on their own in the future.

I always looked forward to reading aloud to my students and my own children. I read bedtime stories to my boys for as long as they would let me. When he was around ten, my middle son announced he was too old for me to be reading him a bedtime story. That night I tucked him in, and went next door to his younger brother's room and began to read his story. At some point little Roger asked a question about something in the book. From the next room over, the answer rang out from middle son Patrick, too old to have a story read to him but still not too old to listen to one read to his little brother.

We all need to hear stories, even after we get big and are fluent, independent readers. My wish is every person could have the pleasure of listening to a story, read or told by someone else.

7

The Power of Old Books

I'm still old-fashioned. I love dusty old books and libraries.

Harper Lee

Once, as the teachers of my elementary school entered the media center for a faculty meeting, we were met by two library carts stacked full of children's books. The media specialist explained she had culled her shelves of old, heavily-used books, and invited us to go through them and take those we felt we could use. The books were pretty grubby, and had been through the hands of many children over the years. Nonetheless, we teachers gathered around and eagerly sifted through the titles. I soon discovered a copy of *The 500 Hats of Bartholomew Cubbins* by Dr. Seuss, copyright 1938, and a 1929 Newbery winner, The *Trumpeter of Krakow* by Eric P. Kelly. I seized upon them with delight.

Both of my newly-acquired books were bound in fabric with dark covers. Their spines were frazzled and shredding, and their corners bowed in and had an appearance of having been dropped, maybe even stood- or sat-upon, many times. Their pages were thin and lay very flat when the book was opened. The books practically opened themselves to certain places, perhaps the best pictures or the most exciting text.

Their pages sported random smudges, rips, and stains - mute testimony to the many turnings and musings in which they had participated.

I have a deep, visceral affection for books like these. They are special to me, not just because so many are well-written and well-illustrated classics, but more precisely because of all the children's hands through which they have passed. Their pages have an odor, a texture, and an appearance that testifies to the places they have been over the years, and the small hands that have turned them and loved them, at times almost to death. As I turn their pages, I see so much evidence of those who have gone before me. The excitement, absorption, delight, and frustration of the former readers have truly penetrated the pages of these books and have added to the vitality of the stories.

I dearly love old books, especially old children's books, both for this atmosphere they bring with them and for the frequent treasures they hide between their bland, homogeneous covers. I often used one old book to teach children the meaning of the saying, "You can't judge a book by its cover." Some years ago I acquired another library discard, an obviously elderly book called *The Pirates' Bridge* by Mary Stuart, copyright 1960. It's dark maroon in color with a plain cloth binding, decorated with a simple picture of a woman and children dressed in turn-of-the-twentieth-century clothing with some pirates in the background. Cardboard peeks through on all four corners and the spine has been repaired more than once. When I pulled it out to read to my students, it was guaranteed to raise a chorus of "We don't want to hear that one. It doesn't look good."

It is, in fact, a delicious old story, featuring brave schoolchildren and their teacher who outwit a band of pirates bent on taking over their one room school. Highly imaginative, totally improbable, thoroughly satisfying. By the time I finished reading it, I'm sure I'd convinced every child in the room of the value of looking beneath the surface - of books and people, too.

So, give me your old, good books any day. Let me catch from them faint whiffs of peanut butter and sweaty palms and library shelf dust. Let me imagine the hands that turned the pages and ran small fingers beneath the words - sporting blisters, Band-Aids, and ragged fingernails, determined to master the mystery of print. Let me feel their soft pages for the magical touch of the power of the burgeoning readers who have gone before me.

The Place for Math Manipulatives in the Classroom

. . . . .

> Math is like ice cream, with more flavors than you can imagine – and if all your children ever do is textbook math, that's like feeding them only broccoli-flavored ice cream.

> Denise Gaskins

The first math manipulatives any child learns to use are his or her fingers. They are a built-in and integral part of our learning to count objects, to understand quantity, and to begin to comprehend the principles of addition and subtraction. I have no doubt humans used their fingers in developing their number sense from the dawn of human history.

I was fortunate to begin my teaching career with young children because it helped me to recognize the essential value of introducing early number concepts with objects that could be held and manipulated. And, as I progressed through teaching kindergartners, then first graders, and then second and third graders I could see that objects we can touch and handle, i.e. manipulatives or hands-on materials, will often give children an essential piece of what is required for them to grasp many math concepts.

Let's take a look at some of the most useful math manipulatives we teachers use:

+ **Counters** –Before there were companies manufacturing items for school children to count, there were primary level teachers collecting and saving countable things. We were good at scrounging through all sorts of discarded and found materials to help us in teaching with manipulatives, but we really hit our stride with counters. We collected buttons, milk caps, nuts, paper clips, old keys, sea shells, anything that could be enumerated. After several years, our schools began purchasing math kits for us that included counters and we were happy to get those - tiny Teddy bears in varying colors, plastic multicolored circles you could see through, and Unifix cubes that could be fastened together. We never really left our found objects behind, though, and, if you walk into a kindergarten or first or second grade classroom even today, you are likely to see a large collection of items that can be used for teaching counting, addition, and subtraction at the most basic level.

+ **Adding machine tape** – This item is a long roll of white, unlined paper 2 ½ inches wide, available at office supply stores. I used adding machine tape all across my white board to write the number of each day of school. I used a long strip of it taped in the middle of the white board to enlist the students' help in making a number line to one hundred. With a number one at the left side and a one hundred on the right we would then estimate where the fifty should go and, from there, place the twenty-five and the seventy-five. Then we could fill in the locations of the fives and make little tick marks for the ones. Another day, we could use this same line for an estimation lesson. I would show the students a clear container full of any item such as marbles, Teddy bear counters, etc. I'd ask them to estimate how many items there were in the container, and here it was important to distinguish between a "wild guess" and an "educated guess," which would be an estimate. They were to write their estimate and their name on a small slip of sticky note. Children would come up to the white board, four or five at a time, to stick the estimate on its correct location on the number line. Then, in front of the class, I would count out around half of the items in the container. I'd record this number on the board and ask if anyone would like to change his or her estimate. This is the moment when you really will have a chance to understand what we mean when we use the term "number sense," that confidence with the concept of quantity which we must all develop if we are to become competent mathematicians. Some children would make a change. They would write a new estimate, place it on that spot on the number line, and remove their old one. Others would sit tight with the number they originally chose. We would then count out the remaining items and notice together, not just the estimate(s) which were spot on, but also those that were close because, after all, this is the whole idea of an estimate, to get *close* to a correct answer. I would point out that in real life, we use estimates more often than exact numbers. We would think of some examples together.

- **The hundred board** – The best hundred board is 11" x 11" in size and is made of heavy, plastic coated paper. In rows of ten the numbers one through one hundred are written on one side while the other side is one hundred blank boxes that can be written on with a dry erase marker. A hundred board is very versatile and can be used to teach counting, understanding of base ten, adding and multiplication, and number patterns. The see-through colored counters partner well with lessons on a hundred board. If you look forward to Chapter 16 with our ten rows of ten different edible objects from the one hundredth day of school, you will see a description of what I felt was the ultimate application of the concept of the hundred board.

- **Money** - By money, I mean real money. There are sets of plastic coins you can acquire, but there is nothing like using real money when it comes to learning how to count coins, and no reason not to use them. Go ahead and give your money a good wash if it will make you feel better. My friend, Joanne McCarthy, a first grade teacher for many years, supplied each of her students with his or her own little bag containing a penny, a nickel, a dime, and a quarter. In order to reduce the chance the money might find its way out of school and to the kid's house, she required each of her students to sign a contract for the coins, acknowledging he or she would replace any of the money if it was lost. Joanne also kept a bag containing coins that ended up on the floor from which she could replenish the student supply when a coin went missing.

  There are quite a lot of good books to help with teaching money skills, among which are *The Purse* by Kathy Caple and *Alexander, Who Used to be Rich Last Sunday* by Judith Viorst. I also had a set of cardboard oversized coins, heads and tails properly illustrated, which afforded a good opportunity to examine the words and images on our coins and their symbolism.

- **Geoboards** – A geoboard is a plastic square with columns and rows of seven pegs (7 X 7). Geobands (rubber bands) can be stretched from peg to peg to make linear shapes – geometric creations or representations of numerals or letters or pictures, and they can be useful for developing eye-hand coordination in young children. I see there is a geoboard app which would be handy if you have concerns about rubber bands zooming around your classroom but, for a child with strong visual or tactile leanings in learning, the real geoboard is a useful tool.

- **Judy clock** – This item is made of wood and is a colorful clock face with clear five minute intervals and one minute marks. The hour and minute hand are synchronized with gears that can be viewed through a clear window so they each move as they would on a real face clock when you move one or the other manually. I don't recommend the small student version of a Judy clock because they don't have synchronized hands. However, I've talked to kindergarten teachers who like to use them for learning to tell time on the hour.

  Here's the place where we have the discussion about whether any child still needs instruction in how to read analog (face) clocks in our digital clock world. The answer is a resounding "yes!" The reason is traditional clocks will teach us about the passage of time in a way that digital clocks cannot. With an analog clock we can gain a visual sense of the movement of the hands to go from one to two minutes or zero to five minutes. How long is a minute? Watch the second hand for sixty seconds. Count as you watch it. You will have a sense of time that you can get in no other way. If you concentrate closely enough, you can even see the clock hands move. As useful as my digital clocks are, I see the comparison between them and analog clocks as similar to the comparison between a GPS and a paper map. Do you want Time's big picture? Look at a face clock.

- **Pattern blocks** – These wonderful wooden blocks come in five different shapes, each shape a different color. Each set contains multiple copies of a regular hexagon, trapezoid, square, 60-degre rhombus, 30-degree rhombus, and equilateral triangle. The mathematical relationships among the pieces provide children with excellent opportunities to learn geometric facts, to study fractions, to build symmetry, to construct and deconstruct complicated patterns, and to develop spatial reasoning skills. And, they are just plain fun to build with too. You may be tempted to use these virtually. They are much more interesting and useful as a hands-on learning tool. A good resource designed to employ pattern blocks with third-sixth graders is *Geometry and Fractions with Pattern Blocks, Grades 3-6* by Barbara Irvin.

+ **Tangrams** – These are another type of geometric shape resource. A tangram set consists of seven pieces - two large triangles, one medium triangle, two small triangles, one square, and one parallelogram. The large triangle is twice the area of the medium triangle. The medium triangle, the square, and the parallelogram are each twice the area of the small triangle. The relationships among the pieces make it possible to put them all together to form a square, which sounds easy but is not. There are many, many possible variations in the ways the pieces relate to each other and the geometric lessons that can be taught with them. A good book to use in introducing the pieces to students is *Grandfather Tang's Story*. As with pattern blocks, there is a teacher resource for grades 3-6 with tangram shapes – *Geometry and Fractions with Tangrams, Grade 3-6*, also by Barbara Irvin. Both the tangram book and the pattern block book can be adapted for use with younger children in many cases.

+ **Unifix cubes** – I mentioned Unifix cubes as an object to help with counting concepts earlier but there are multiple other ways to employ them. The cubes are plastic 3D one-inch squares that lock together securely on one side and come apart with a snap. They come in eight different bright colors, and black and white. You can teach counting by twos by linking two in one color, then two of another, and so on. You can teach counting by fives and tens and any other number by grouping the colors appropriately. You can divide your students into teams by putting colored cubes in a bag and having kids each draw one cube out of the bag and then grouping themselves by color. You can help your students learn the concept of patterns and you can link different colored cubes to make math facts. Different colored cubes can be used to designate different data for graphing. They can be used for measurement and to show multiplication facts.

+ **Base ten blocks** – Base ten blocks are a plastic manipulative that come in small cube units, ten cube-sized rods (making ten units), ten rod-sized flats (making one hundred units) and ten flat-sized blocks (making 1000 units). Lines are marked on each piece to designate units. This is a versatile tool for kindergarten-fifth grade students, helping with counting, with grouping into sets of ten, with understanding place value, and skills of multi-digit addition and subtraction. Their one big handicap from the point of view of a primary level teacher is the size of the basic unit. It is a centimeter square and so small it's easy for them to get scattered and lost. I like them, though, for the third through fifth graders who will benefit from being able to count the units and clearly see the sequence from ones to tens to hundreds to thousands as they work on understanding place value.

+ **Ten frame** – A ten frame is a five by two arrangement of squares or cups on which children can practice number relationships for numbers up to ten. You can use plastic counting disks, which are one color on one side and a different color on the other and, for instance, represent 3 + 2 with three of one color in the first column, and two of the other color in the second column. You could also act out subtraction problems with the frame and transfer that visual relationship to paper.

+ **Fraction kits** – (See directions in the Appendix for how to make your own.) You can use these kits to introduce basic fractions, to recognize fractions are a part of a whole, to create equivalent fractions, and to compare fractions. Early on in fraction introduction, I read fractions as "one of two equal parts" for ½, "one of four equal parts" for ¼, "five of eight equal parts" for 5/8, etc. This helps to firmly establish in a student's brain the notion that a fraction represents part of a whole whose parts are divided equally.

Two of the best authors who guided me in employing hands-on materials to teach children math are Mary Baratta-Lorton and Marilyn Burns. Baratta-Lorton wrote *Mathematics Their Way* and *Workjobs: Activity-Centered Learning for Early Childhood Education*. Her focus is on the use of multi-sensory experiences to teach mathematics and language skills in early elementary grades. Marilyn Burns' career has spanned more than fifty years, and she guided me through many a math lesson as I worked to make math make sense to my students. One of her many books, *About Teaching Mathematics*, is a valuable resource for teaching math through problem solving to students K-8.

I highly recommend you find a video of Marilyn Burns teaching a class. She's a great inspiration as she encourages children to reason their way through a mathematics challenge and waits patiently for them to develop solutions. She, more than any other fellow educator, taught me the value of giving children time to think. Ask a question – wait, wait, wait – and validate the answer. Two other books by Burns that I went back to again and again are *Math for Smarty Pants* and *The I Hate Mathematics! Book*. On one occasion Burns was speaking at a math convention I attended. She happened to get into an elevator occupied by some colleagues and me. We were tongue-tied and awestruck, and could not think of anything to say to her. You would have thought she was a rock star, which of course, to us, she was.

Getting Along With Each Other

· ○ ● ◦ ●

"You've got to be taught to hate."
From the Broadway musical *South Pacific*

by Rodgers and Hammerstein, 1949

C hildren are not born with hatred or prejudice in their hearts. As the song from the Broadway musical, *South Pacific*, says in its title, "You've got to be carefully taught." I could see this first-hand in my life as a teacher. The younger the children I interacted with were, the more color-blind and culture-blind they were. They learned prejudice from their families and from the society around them. Without a serious effort to prevent that or to change them, it only hardened as they got older.

When I was a young child, my grandmother had a Black man who did her yard work one day each week. At lunchtime she fed Wilson lunch at a table on her back porch. I liked Wilson and wanted to eat lunch with him, and was totally puzzled that my grandmother relegated him to the back porch to eat, and wouldn't let me join him, not realizing until I was much older that it was all about the color of his skin.

I was a high school senior in 1965, and my mother was the president of my junior-senior high school's Parent-Teacher Association that year. The school was located in a deeply segregated Southern town, but that school year it was integrated for the first time with twelve seventh grade Black children who were bused in to join us. I can't imagine how difficult it was for those kids to become a tiny part of the lowest grade at a 1,000 student school. My mother knew it would be difficult for them, and one way she tried to help was by personally inviting each of their parents to join the PTA. I'm sure she was met with criticism and resistance in doing that by other parents in the community. But she was a stubborn woman and she did not back down.

In spite of the 1964 Civil Rights Act, which prohibited employment discrimination on the basis of race, color, religion, sex, or national origin, racism in the United States persists to this day. Over the course of my teaching career, I worked in schools with mostly white children and schools with mostly Black children, but I never worked in a school where the proportions of children of each race mirrored that of the larger society, where the children were coming from truly integrated neighborhoods. Integration in America was supposed to happen when white children and Black children began going to school together, but there was very little effort to help integration take hold in the larger society. It's as though we lay the burden of integration solely on the backs of our children, with little to no understanding that their parents had to be enlisted in the effort too.

How do you encourage and promote equitable racial and cultural attitudes in your classroom? I think the starting point is established in those first few days when you make up your class list of rules. "Treat other people the way you want them to treat you" is a statement ripe for classroom discussion. Children can imagine themselves in a difficult situation – being left out of a game, having no one to sit with at lunch, being bullied on the bus. Make it a point to ask these questions: "How would you feel if one of these situations happened to you?" "How can you help someone who is the victim in one of those situations?" and, more important, "Would you help someone who is being isolated or bullied?" These discussions should be honest and up-front in your classroom, and not only should they begin to be asked early in the school year, they should continue throughout the year. They're not easy conversations to have, but even kindergartners can think about them.

What is your role as a teacher? First of all, honestly examine yourself for racial bias and stereotypes. Do you expect less from children of color? Do you call on your Black children less often when they raise a hand to answer? Do you find yourself excusing minority children from your high expectation of other children? Be honest in your examination of yourself, whether you are white or Black or Latino or Asian.

Two books had a profound impact in helping me in my self-examination of my racial attitudes – *Black Like Me* by John Howard Griffin, and *Savage Inequalities* by Jonathan Kozol. I read Griffin's book when I was a teenager. He was a journalist from Texas, who wanted to know what it was like to be Black in America. In 1959, under the care of a dermatologist, he took medication and exposed himself to ultraviolet light until his skin was dark enough that he could pass as an African American. Then he traveled throughout the Deep South for six weeks. The diary he kept during his travels formed the basis of his book as he discovered firsthand the deep differences between treatment of white people in America and Black people in America.

Jonathan Kozol published *Savage Inequalities* in 1991. In 1988, he began a journey to visit several of America's largest cities, both in the North and in the South. A quarter of a century after the 1964 Civil Right Act, he found the act's prohibition of racial segregation in schools was an empty promise. As he traveled through East St Louis, the South side of Chicago, New York City, Camden, New Jersey, Washington, DC, and San Antonio, Texas, Kozol observed and wrote about inner city schools in all sorts of conditions of decay, children who lacked good teachers, and a deplorable scarcity of good materials for learning. Now, thirty years after his book was written, so many of the same conditions still exist in our country. What can we do to make things better? As a teacher you can be an agent of change in your classroom.

I've known several fourth and fifth grade teachers who helped their students understand the impact of discrimination through a simple classroom exercise. As students arrive in the classroom for the day, the teacher directs those with light colored eyes to sit at seats in the back of the room, and sends students with dark eyes to sit at the front with no explanation of her reason for placing them thus. Over the course of about an hour, the teacher hands out materials to the dark-eyed students first, and makes a subtle point of calling on the dark eyed students more often as she proceeds with instruction. At some point, she mentions students will be going to the hallway water fountains for a drink, but she lets the dark-eyed students go first; then she tells the rest of the class that time is short and they'll have to wait until later. It never takes very long for the light-eyed students to begin to feel like they are being badly treated and, of course, it makes for a fruitful class discussion of how that feels, linking the lesson to how such discrimination has affected our country.

As always, I find myself turning to literature to help students understand and discuss societal issues of importance. Robert Munsch, author, and Michael Martchenko, illustrator, collaborated on several books I would recommend for exploring cultural and racial differences: *From Far Away*, by Munsch and Saoussan Askar, tells the true story of seven-year-old Saoussan who immigrated to Canada from war torn Lebanon, and how she navigates living in a new home, learning a new language, and building confidence after the trauma of war.

Munsch's talents for telling exaggerated, over-the-top stories which appeal to the funny bone in kindergartners through third graders is evident in *Angela's Airplane* and *David's Father* and *Something Good*. All three of these books are populated with light and dark-skinned people, comfortably interacting together, and each of the three has a gentle lesson to be taught and discussed.

For upper elementary aged students, I have several favorites: *Tall Grass* by Sandra Dallas is an eloquent story about the removal of Japanese-American citizens to internment camps during World War

II. *The Watsons Go to Birmingham* by Christopher Paul Curtis is a fictional story, but it references an historical event in 1963 during the civil rights movement. *Remember My Name* by Sara Banks is a book about a friendship between two children who are affected by the forced removal of Native Americans from Georgia in 1838.

In my experience, children have a keen sense of right and wrong, fair and unfair. When we give them an opportunity to think about and talk about societal injustices, we open them up to the possibility they'll carry class discussions on with them into their homes, into their futures, and maybe, just maybe, they will become the instruments of change that make the world a better place.

10

What my Friend George Taught me About Teaching

Children are given to us - on loan - for a very short period of time. They come to us like packets of flower seeds, with no pictures on the cover and no guarantees. We do not know what they will look like, act like, or have the potential to become. Our job, like the gardener's, is to meet their needs as best we can: to give proper nourishment, love, attention, and care, and to hope for the best.

Katharine Kersey

When I was growing up, I had a next-door neighbor friend named George Winston. Our families remained friends even after we both moved to other states. George was an odd little character, and probably the first highly gifted child I ever knew, although I certainly didn't understand that at the time. He had numerous talents and an active imagination which led him into many varied directions. He delved deeply into any topic of interest to him, and he was willing to play with me and other kids in the neighborhood, but only when we were willing to go along with whatever was interesting him at the time.

One year, while I was teaching at Conway, I had a student much like George. Richard was bright and, when I introduced a topic of study that captured his interest, he would dig into it with enthusiasm. If what I wanted him to learn didn't interest him, though, he just tuned me out. I was pretty frustrated and exasperated with this situation, and fretted over what to do to solve it.

About midway through the year, my childhood friend George's mother got in touch with me. It seemed, in adulthood, George had become a professional musician, and was coming to Orlando to perform. George's mom invited my husband and me to join her and George's dad at his concert. I was interested to see George again, and wanted to support someone I assumed was a struggling musician. Imagine my surprise when we arrived at the city auditorium to find it packed with fans of George.

When my childhood friend walked out on stage, and took his place at the piano, and began to play truly beautiful music, I had a moment of both surprise and understanding. I realized what my student Richard needed more than anything else was space and acceptance of the person he was, the chance to grow into his talents, and to be nurtured in such a way that his gifts could develop. Richard was not going to fit into the mold of "typical kindergartner." Indeed, the best part of Richard would be lost if I tried to fit him into that mold. I decided to appreciate Richard for who he was, to be patient with him during the times when he seemed to be balking at things I asked him to do, and to enjoy his own special brand of personality. I anticipated looking forward to the day when I might learn that he too, having been given the freedom to develop his gifts and talents, was delighting millions of people with his delicious imagination, and his own particular brand of zest for life.

This is what all children need, whether they are highly gifted or not. I truly began to understand that my job as a teacher was to try my best to help my students realize and develop the talents and gifts they brought with them into my classroom.

Supervising New Teachers

• • • • •

The dream begins with a teacher who believes in you,
who tugs and pushes and leads you to the next plateau,
sometimes poking you with a sharp stick called truth.

Dan Rather

In 1987, I had the chance to be a supervising teacher for an exchange teacher from Beijing, China. Our teacher came to us through the American Field Service exchange program to work at Conway Elementary in my classroom, and be a resource about life in modern-day China, both at my school and throughout Orange County. She was an interesting young woman and taught me many things, maybe much more than I taught her.

On one occasion, our class was preparing to study fables and folk tales from around the world. Thinking our Chinese teacher would enjoy being our resource for Chinese folk tales, I asked her to prepare some lessons on folk tales she knew. She surprised me by saying, "I do not know any Chinese folk tales." I was a little startled by her remark. Then I thought about what she had said, and eventually realized her childhood had occurred during the height of China's Cultural Revolution, a period when the China's leaders were busily discarding and denigrating the old ways as they led the population into

Communist rule. How sad she wasn't even allowed to learn China's years of rich folk tales.

I was a supervising teacher during four terms for teacher interns over the course of my years at Conway. I always tried to remember the lessons I'd learned from my own supervising teachers and experienced colleagues. I feel strongly a teacher's internship period is probably the most valuable part of his or her teacher training period. In the best of all possible arrangements, an intern spends the fall quarter of the school year in internship so she or he has the chance to see how the school routine is set up, rules established, and learning centers organized, all of which are very valuable parts of learning to be a teacher.

I tried to provide ample feedback to my interns, with lots of explanation for why I was doing the things I did in the classroom, and exposure to good lessons and ideas that my student teacher could carry into his or her own future classroom. Ideally, an intern begins by observing in the classroom for several weeks. Gradually, she or he is given more and more responsibility for lesson planning and teaching until, around the last month of the term, the intern assumes responsibility for teaching the class full-time. In the best possible schedule, the intern has about a week at the end of his or her internship to observe in other classrooms at the school, and to interact with other teachers.

During the periods while I had my interns, I tried to make an opportunity to film my student teacher in action. It's so valuable to watch yourself teach - to see whether you tend to focus your attention on one side of the room, to notice if you're not writing large enough on the board for the kids in the back row to see, to realize your voice is too quiet for everyone to hear. All of these are things you want to know about and correct before you're dropped into your own classroom with no one nearby to rescue you. One time I asked my student teacher to film me. It was very enlightening, especially when the filming revealed that one of my "best" students had perfected a technique of appearing to be totally engrossed in the lesson, while all the while her hands were busy playing with toys she had stashed in her desk.

Another time I had an intern who performed so poorly I suggested to her college's supervising professor that the aspiring teacher should be steered into another career field. This was met with strong opposition on the part of the college. After she left me, I often worried about the students with whom she would cross paths in the future. The time to keep a bad teacher out of the classroom is, hopefully, before he or she ever gets in there.

As much as I enjoyed the chance to guide and influence a new teacher, that moment when I handed the class over to the student teacher was *hard*. Maybe it's similar to the feeling an airplane pilot has in handing the controls over to a student pilot. *Can she be trusted? Will he crash and burn? Will there be irreparable damage done to "my" students?* It was hard, but inspiring and satisfying to watch an intern competently and confidently take control and, with his or her own style, do the things necessary to make learning happen.

12

Meeting the Needs of Students with Learning Disabilities

• ◦ ● ◦ •

If a child can't learn the way we teach, maybe we should teach the way they learn.

Ignacio Estrada

When my husband, Wayne, was a third grader in 1954, he went home one day in tears. That day he had been assigned to the slow reading group. Wayne knew he was a smart kid. He was good in math and science, but he struggled to read. Being put into that reading group, where he knew he was with other children having serious academic problems, was devastating to him. He didn't realize he had atypical reading problems until he was placed in that group. Being in the slow reading group did not solve his reading problems, and the rest of his school years were spent laboriously trudging through assigned texts.

As a fifth grader, he became interested in dinosaurs and found a book, *All About Dinosaurs*, in his school library. He checked it out, and took it home, and only managed to read his way through ten or fifteen pages over the space of two weeks. Then the book was due and he had to return it. Even with a deep interest in the world around him - airplanes, trains, electricity - the *All About* books had stumped him and before long, he stopped checking books out from the library.

Wayne went on in later years to earn an engineering degree from Georgia Tech, but he never read for pleasure, and he labored over the chapters assigned to him in high school and college. One day, not long after we married, he watched as I finished reading a novel. I set it down and said, "That was a good book."

"I saw you start that book two days ago. You haven't read the entire book in that time, have you?" Wayne asked.

I had, and he told me there was no way he could have made it through that book in anything under a month, nor would he have chosen to do so. Reading was so hard for him that, with the exception of magazine articles, he never read. He told me how he had been fascinated to learn things in books as a child, but couldn't get the lines to stay still as he read. He would read a line but, as he went down the page, he'd find he was reading the same line over and over.

What he said made me want to cry. Wayne is smart and capable. He is a problem solver of the first order. He is a builder and a mechanic, a gifted designer and a repairman of everything that can possibly break. He became all of those things without being a fluent reader in an era when reading disabilities were not recognized or understood. Nor did I, at that time, realize Wayne probably possessed a reading disability.

Years later, I found research on different learning modalities proposing that people learn in different styles. Some absorb information best through their listening skills, while others' strength is in visual learning, and even others are physical and tactile learners. Although they were not diagnosed or treated in their time as learning disabled, there is evidence to suggest that Albert Einstein, Thomas Edison, and Leonardo da Vinci learned in unconventional ways that made formal schooling difficult or even inappropriate for them. In modern times, famous personalities such as Henry Winkler, Whoopi Goldberg, and Steven Spielberg have revealed their own struggles with learning to read.

I can certainly see my husband is much more of a tactile learner. I could see these different strengths in my young students too, and this caused me to try to approach teaching from different angles in order to reach the students who were more strongly auditory or tactile learners. I could also see that often children who had reading difficulties were intellectually strong in other areas of study and/or in their general intellectual strengths.

When it comes to reading, though, we have to face the fact that learning to read is a survival skill. By the time I had been teaching for several years, I began to see students who had reading difficulties that reminded me of my husband's reading problems. I noticed that among kindergartners it was not unusual for five- and six-year-olds to reverse letters. I'm reminded of a kindergartner who one day proudly showed me how she had printed her first and last names perfectly - backwards.

Lower case B (b) and D (d) and P (p) and Q (q) presented many children with difficulties as we worked on lower case recognition skills. Another teacher showed me an effective way to help kids with this. I would demonstrate that if we formed a circle of our left thumb and forefinger and held the rest of our fingers upright, the circle we made would be on the same side as it is on the stick of the b. If we formed the circle with our right thumb and forefinger and held our right hand fingers upright, we had what looked like a d. Since, when we say the alphabet, the letter "b" comes before the letter "d," we can remember our left hand (coming before our right) is the b and our right is the d. The same point can be made with p and q, imagining our arms as the stick on the letter and remembering that alphabetically "p" comes before "q."

Most students soon internalize this trick and don't need to employ their fingers and a quiet recitation of the alphabet as a reminder. The child who still needs it as a late first or second grader would be a red flag for me to be tuned into whether reading difficulties are developing that could need further assessment, and perhaps cuing me to be prepared to help with more one-on-one attention or with different strategies.

Whatever the cause, I know that perceptual problems with letter shapes can turn reading into a demoralizing encounter with a line of print.

Some of my students had trouble perceiving how the letter sounds in a word blended together to make the word. They could learn and remember individual letter sounds in isolation but, when tasked with putting each sound together to create a word, they just could not seem to do the blending necessary to make it happen. And, of course, the longer the word, the harder the task. By the time the child had laboriously sounded out the word, the entire memory of the passage being read had disappeared. How discouraging! You can see how this problem can easily lead to difficulties retelling what has been read, problems with deep understanding of a reading assignment, and difficulty with making inferences about a passage.

Sometimes I could address this problem by concentrating on helping the child learn what we call "sight words." These are the many basic words that occur over and over in print. Practicing reading and remembering these words - by posting them prominently in the classroom and reading them aloud often and by sending them home for daily practice, even over the summer, can give some students the basic tools to build on with more difficult words.

Spelling words correctly can pose frustrating problems for students with a reading disability. Thank goodness for spell check on our computers, something we did not have in the "old days." Back then, a child was faced with trying to look up a word whose first and second letters may have been obvious, but whose remaining sounds were elusive and, therefore, a difficult chore to search out in the dictionary. Think about what a huge barrier to reading and writing it is to be stymied at every turn with the inability to spell correctly!

Some children have trouble with their working memory: the ability to hold and manipulate information in the moment. This problem can spill over into math learning as well and can be seen as a disability in this area of study.

Documenting a child's learning difficulties, and bringing them to the attention of parents and school specialists, is key to developing strategies to help students who have trouble reading. Whatever tools we can offer to the reader who experiences problems will be an essential part of that kid's education. Oddly, or maybe it's not so odd, I often found a familial connection when I had a student with a reading problem. If I asked the parents if either of them had experienced trouble learning to read, frequently the father acknowledged he had. And almost as frequently, it had not been addressed.

It goes without saying that a child who finds frustration in his or her school experience often demonstrates it with anger or withdrawal or loss of interest in learning, if not all three. This child may come to think of himself or herself as "stupid" or mentally deficient, and may just give up on learning. There is a wonderful book by Patricia Polacco, *Thank you, Mr. Falker*, which tells of the author's own experience with a sensitive teacher who found the way to lead her to reading. Our job as teachers is to be observant enough to notice early on what is happening, and to employ the resources to help.

13

Connecting Math With Literature

· ∘ ● ∘ ·

When we find a way to weave literature into math the line between "good" readers and "good" mathematicians begins to blur.

Colleen Thrailkill

While I was teaching second grade in 1993, I wrote and was funded with a grant from the Mathematics Education Trust to purchase books to link math and literature. I was realizing there were many opportunities to integrate these two important subjects in school. The not-so-able reader could easily be my star math student, and the child who consumed every book in sight might also be my floundering math kid. Why not mix the two subjects together and see what happened?

There were multiple resources available to help a teacher to do this, with titles such as *Literature-Based Math Activities: An Integrated Approach* by Alison Abrohms, *Books You Can Count On: Linking Mathematics and Literature* by Margaret Clyne and Rachel Griffiths, and *Math and Literature (K-3)* by Marilyn Burns and Stephanie Sheffield. There was a wealth of books for elementary students, high quality and interesting stories that bring a math element into their telling. I spent several months researching to find the books I wanted. I talked to colleagues, looked in bookstores, consulted with librarians, and attended a National Council of Teachers of Mathematics conference where I scoured the vendors to help me spend my grant money. I managed to spend every cent of it.

Then I began reading and organizing the titles into the math topics and appropriate grade levels for the books I found. I could tie a story in with teaching children how to tell time, understanding fractions, learning money skills, or geometry activities. For almost every area of study I touched on with kindergarten through third grade students, I could find a good book to help me, or to recommend to another teacher.

Here are a few of the books I selected, the grade levels they are most appropriate for (mostly K-3), and the skills they can help you to teach:

+ The story "A Lost Button" from *Frog and Toad are Friends* by Arnold Lobel can help you teach discrimination among attributes. Grades K-2

+ *The Doorbell Rang* by Pat Hutchins will give an introduction to simple division. Grades K-2

+ *Round Trip* by Ann Jonas is a clever use of black and white optical illusions to help with developing spatial sense. Grades 1-3

+ *Caps for Sale* by Esphyr Slobodkina is a basic counting book with a twist involving monkeys that kindergartners and first graders can't resist. Grades K-1

+ "Smart," a poem by Shel Silverstein in *Where the Sidewalk Ends* works well to show money subtraction skills and is also very funny. Grades 2-3

+ *How Big is a Foot?* by Rolf Myller will help to set you on your way in a linear measuring unit. Grades K-2

- *The Twelve Days of Christmas,* Hilary Knight's rendition of the old carol is a chance for some big number addition as students calculate just how many gifts were given altogether in the twelve days. Grades 2-3

- *Grandfather Tang's Story* by Ann Tompert is an introduction to tangram puzzle pieces leading into some good lessons in plane geometry. This book can be used differently on several different levels. Grades K-5

- *The Napping House* by Audrey Wood is a nice introduction to basic addition. I also turned it into a simple multiplication and addition lesson by having children calculate the number of feet for all the people and animals who lived in the house in the book. Then we would each make our own origami napping house (directions in the Appendix). After you make the house, have students open the doors on their origami house and draw stick figures of everyone who lives in their own house, including pets. Be prepared for the "Are goldfish included?" question and, "How many legs are on my pet spider?" You also may have to address a situation where a sibling is away at college or a parent is away in the military. Come to a reasonable settlement with which everyone can agree. This is not a contest to see who has the most feet. Children should put a name on every stick figure to make sure everyone is accounted for, then write an adding sentence to see how many feet there are in all at their own house. Share to see how much variety you have. You could also have students write different number sentences for the two-legged and the four-legged members of the family and compare those. Grades K-2

- *Gator Pie* by Louise Mathews is the most graphic and easily understandable book I ever found for illustrating dividing a circle into halves, thirds, fourths, eighths and hundredths. Grades 1-3

In the years since I went on my hunt for math/literature treasures, I have no doubt many more books like these have been written. And now you have the Internet to help you to find them, and all kinds of resources to help you track them down and buy them. And I have no doubt there are grants out there to give you the money to pay for them. Go for it!

14

Some Kids Just Stick in Your Head

· · • · ·

It is easier to build strong children than to repair broken men.

Often attributed to Frederick Douglas

Memories of so many students stick with teachers, long after the children have left their classrooms. At Conway Elementary there was Julia, the best girl for the job. Around 1996, I was teaching third graders, and we were preparing to produce a class play. It was titled *Stone Soup: A Rock Opera* by Kaplan-Lyss and Becker, and was a musical adaptation of the old story I had used as a cooking lesson in earlier grades. In the course of discussing the roles in the play and the parts students wanted to perform, Julia spoke up and said she would like to play the part of one of the soldiers. Several boys in the class piped up and said those parts had to be played by boys. I told them girls could be soldiers too and that Julia could be considered for the part if she wanted. She got the part and stole the show. It was an excellent lesson for the entire class in the reality that sometimes the best man for a job is a woman.

One of several of our Stone Soup productions

One year in January, my students had a writing assignment to write about a favorite holiday gift they had received. Jared wrote about getting a great pair of knees. I was perplexed and asked him to tell me more. He said the gift he got was a new puppy and that the breed was called a great pair of knees. Now I was totally flummoxed. I sent him to Volume D in our classroom set of encyclopedia and asked him if he could find a picture of his new pet. It didn't take long for him to show me a likeness – a Great Pyrenees puppy, a dog breed that was totally new to me.

A teacher friend of mine who taught first grade in St. Louis, Missouri, remembers one of her student stories: "I wore glasses and didn't have to always have them on. I tried wearing them across the top of my head so they were handy. Many times the glasses would fall off and, being busy, I would just lay them down, wherever. Then, of course, I would forget where I was the last place those glasses were laid. 'Alert everyone! I have lost my glasses again.' The whole class would stop and look around and locate the glasses. This was not just a random occurrence, but a daily occurrence".

"One day I noticed one of my students had her head lowered when my glasses had gone missing again. Thinking she was ill, I went over to her. 'Are you okay?' I asked. She answered, 'I am praying that we find your glasses.'"

Not every experience we have with our students is a good one. Back when I was teaching second grade, I had a student named Alex. I arranged to do his home visit in October and arrived at his house as scheduled. His mother answered the door, invited me to sit down in the living room and proceeded to launch into complaints about her son, my student. I could see Alex was mortified and embarrassed, and I was too. I quickly told Alex's mother that I wasn't there for a parent conference, and I would like to have Alex show me his room and his favorite toys.

We walked down the hall to a tiny bedroom, with this very unmotherly mother trailing along behind us, continuing to itemize all the failings of her seven-year-old son. Alex and I did the best we could to carry on our visit and not listen to her. My visit certainly gave me new insight and understanding into some of problems Alex had that were spilling over into our classroom. Children spend a large part of their days in school, but they may be going back to horribly challenging and difficult situations after they leave us.

And then there was Edward. He was one of my first graders and lived with his father and grandparents. One day when we were having Show and Tell, Edward reported his uncle was out of jail and now living with his family. I said something like, "That's nice. I'm sure you're happy to have him around."

Edward's brief reply was "Not really."

Several weeks passed and I began to notice a change in Edward's behavior. He had gone from a sweet, sociable little kid to a bit of an aggressor. One day, as we walked to the cafeteria, I saw him grab at the front of another little boy's pants.

I pulled him aside and said, "Edward, it's not okay for you to do that to someone. Nobody does that to you."

"Yes, they do," he said.

"Who does it to you?" I asked.

"My uncle."

I was stunned. I walked Edward and the rest of the students to the cafeteria and went, on shaking legs, to tell my principal what Edward had said. He immediately called and reported what I'd been told to the authorities. By the next day, a social worker came to school to interview Edward and I insisted upon sitting in on the interview so Edward would not be speaking to a stranger with no one he knew present. He confirmed what he had said to me earlier. In the end, the uncle was forbidden to have contact with Edward. Did that make everything all right? I don't know.

One year I was assigned a second grader who was living in foster care. I knew only that he had come from a difficult situation, and I soon realized he was a child in serious distress. He was unable to interact with the other students, and spent most of his days with us crawling under classroom tables, screaming uncontrollably, and even trying to run away from the school. Several weeks went by and nothing I tried to do to help him worked. Finally one day - during a particularly violent moment on his part - I took him outside the classroom door to give him a chance to calm down.

I forced him to look into my eyes and I said, "I know things are really bad for you right now. If I could fix all those bad things I would, but I can't. But one thing I can promise you: I will do everything in my power to make school a safe place for you."

Did that help? I had no way of knowing. He was soon moved to another school and I never heard any more about him.

Children bring a lot of baggage with them into the classroom. I once had the mother of a student confide to me at the beginning of the school year that she was dying, and would likely not be alive by Thanksgiving. I've had multiple students who came from homes where they are living in devastating situations. No teacher can be unaffected by the tragedies that happen to her or his students. Often, we can't help but take these heartaches home with us. With the passage of many years in the classroom, I have had to come to the difficult realization that, while I would do everything in my power to make school a safe and secure place for my students, I couldn't fix everything wrong in their lives. But I would do all it was possible for me to do. That's the way it is with all of life's challenges. All we can do is our best.

15

Teaching With Quilts

· · • · ·

So her mother rocked her as mothers do. Then she tucked her in. And she felt at home again under the quilt.

The Quilt Story by Tony Johnston & Tomie dePaola

My paternal grandmother was a prolific quilter, and our family made good use of the quilts she made for us. They were all hand stitched and stuffed with wool from the sheep on her Montana farm. I was fascinated with the mathematics of the shapes in quilts, and on several occasions used traditional quilt patterns when I taught geometry and measurement.

While I was teaching second graders at Conway Elementary, I used a resource book titled *Math Excursions 2* by Donna Burk, Allyn Snider, and Paula Symonds. This was one in the authors' three book series using project-based mathematics. *Math Excursions 2* was geared toward second graders and offered children the chance to explore simple and complicated patterns of quilt blocks, among several other projects.

To begin our quilt pattern project, we read picture books about quilting, and looked at some real quilts, and told the stories behind their making. A few of the books we enjoyed together were *The Quilt Story* by Tony Johnston, *The Keeping Quilt* by Patricia Polacco, *The Quiltmaker's Gift* by Jeff Brumbeau, and *Reuben and the Quilt* by Merle Good.

Next, I cut out hundreds of two-inch squares from gold foil Christmas wrapping paper and red, blue, and green construction paper Then, organized in groups of two or three, my students followed a picture guide to arrange the squares in a set pattern on an 18" square of white paper. It was not an easy task. It took careful work and group cooperation as well as fine attention to details for each group to properly glue down their 64 squares in the right places. When each group was finished, one group at a time, the students glued our nine 16" squares to a huge 48" x 48" piece of paper. Our resulting design was a replica of a traditional quilting pattern called "Trip Around the World" and it was spectacular, as large as a real quilt would be. The use of the gold wrapping paper was a nice touch, adding glamour and glitz.

As a class we felt a lot of satisfaction at completing this project. As a teacher I was pleased my students had learned some linear measurement skills, some important properties of squares, and had some exposure to perimeter and area calculation, not to mention the chance for a touch of multiplying and an excellent opportunity for teamwork.

Our "Trip Around the World" Quilt

With third graders I had another quilting lesson I felt was valuable. We read a collection of stories about quilts, and examined different traditional quilt designs. We invited a quilter to come and speak to the class. She taught us about complementary colors, how quilters plan their quilting creations, and introduced us to basic quilters' language. She showed us some of the quilts she had made, and we talked about whether we had quilts that were made for us by a family member. I showed my students a quilt my Montana grandmother had made for me when I was a baby, and several students showed quilts that were made for them.

Then I cut out a lot of four-inch squares of two different colors of construction paper. I gave each student four of the squares in two different colors and a sheet of white paper cut to eight inches square. We discussed the dimensions of the colored squares and then I asked the students to place the squares in such a way that they covered all of the eight-inch square. There are only a limited number of ways to do this and we quickly discovered and discussed them all.

Then I had the kids carefully fold their squares on the diagonal and carefully cut them to end up with eight triangles, four in each color. Again, I asked them to use all their paper pieces to cover the eight-inch square so there was no white paper showing. Many more designs emerged and we had the chance to talk about how we had changed our squares into triangles, how many triangles it took to make each square, and the relationships among the shapes we were working with. I asked the students to each create a few different designs they liked with the triangles, and then to decide on an arrangement they liked best and glue it in place.

We looked, and marveled, at the great variety of designs we now had. Some that we thought were different could be made to be the same with a flip or a turn. We discussed mirror images, and could manipulate our squares to see similarities and differences among our designs. We talked about symmetry, and had a discussion about fractions. Each student gave his or her quilt block an original name, which was written on the back of the block, and we displayed the blocks on a bulletin board, deciding as we placed them if somewhere among all we had made we had a matching one. I felt this chance to exercise spatial reasoning in this activity was just as valuable as the geometry of shapes we studied.

I hope my students were enriched by the multiple aspects of this unit, from our appreciation of quilts past and present, to our study of geometry, and our exposure to the thought that goes into creating a quilt.

Since those days of making paper quilts and quilt blocks, I have become a fabric quilter, just like my grandmother, though I don't have my own sheep to supply me with wool. In later years, when I shared the triangle quilt block lesson, I also shared a few of the quilts I made and my passion for appreciating the patterns quilts reveal.

An Attic Window quilt I made in 2020

16

The One Hundredth Day of School

- - • - -

There should be no such thing as boring mathematics.

Edsger Dijkstra

One of my favorite math lessons happened each year on the one hundredth day of the school year. I first celebrated this important milestone with second graders in 1991. One hundred is a magical number for kids. Remember, if you can, your own pride when you were first able to successfully count all the way to one hundred. The one hundredth day usually occurs in early- to mid-February in the school year. By this time second graders are expected to have a good number sense for numbers from zero to ninety-nine. Teachers are developing an understanding of place value with their students, preparing them to do two-digit addition and subtraction that will involve regrouping.

In my classroom, we had an adding machine tape running along the top edge of the chalkboard. Each school day we wrote the number of that day in the school year. Every time we reached a ten, I wrote it in red, without explaining the significance early on. On our classroom calendar display, we had a set of three pockets, labeled ones, tens, hundreds. Each day, as we went over the date first thing in the morning, we put a Popsicle stick in the ones pocket. Every time we reached ten sticks in the ones pocket, we would bundle that set with a rubber band and "trade" it for a single stick we placed in the tens pocket. When we had ten sticks in the tens pocket, we bundled that set and "traded" it for one stick in the hundreds pocket. We would write and read the number we had created each day. By the time we began to close in on the hundredth day, we were all excited and planned a big celebration for the big day itself. On the one hundredth day, we added a glittery number one hundred to the adding machine number line above the chalkboard.

Over multiple years and multiple one hundredth day celebrations with my second grade students, here are some of the things we did: we made pop-up Happy Hundred greeting cards; we estimated if one hundred kernels of corn would be enough to pop for a class, and popped and ate the popcorn to find the answer; we thought of one hundred words to write; we had a contest to see who could get the largest number in one hundred seconds by repeatedly adding 1 on a calculator; we cooked happy hundred chicken noodle soup made with short, straight noodles for ones and circle noodles for zeros. (Check the Appendix for the recipe.) We thought of words we could make from the letters in the words "one hundred," and we glued uncooked spaghetti and macaroni to outline the number one hundred on a sign.

After I moved to third grade, the activities grew more challenging, including the following: we drew a picture of how we would look when we reached one hundred years of age; we estimated which of three bundles of sticks, three trains of Unifix cubes, and three jars of jelly beans held exactly one hundred; we read the book *101 Dalmatians* and, of course, counted *all* the dogs on the final page. One year, I challenged my third graders to figure out where the minute hand would be when we reached the one hundredth minute of our school day on the one hundredth day. It turned out the clock would read 10:00 a.m. at that moment. Honestly, I did not plan that. At 10:00 a.m. exactly, we all went outside, and each one of us popped a balloon, and loudly shouted "Happy Hundred!" In one activity, I gave each table group one hundred pattern blocks, and asked them to make a group design using all of the blocks. Each table group then toured the room to see all the creations. Students thought up and wrote one hundred words. There is a nice selection of books on the market about the hundredth day of school, and one I like is *100th Day Worries* by Margery Cuyler.

The most fun of all the one hundredth day celebrations, though, was making an edible hundred chart. Besides being fun, I saw this activity as a great way to build my students' number sense, and to begin building their understanding of place value. First, we all washed and dried our hands. I had gathered a bunch of edibles, like Cheerios, raisins, tiny pretzels, M&Ms, Chex cereal squares, dried cranberries, chocolate chips, red hot candies, and miniature marshmallows. Then, at the top of a piece of waxed paper each child had, we made a row of ten of one of the edible items—and wrote the number "10" with a marker beside that row. The next row was made of ten of a different edible item, with "20" written beside that row. We continued in this fashion all the way to the bottom row of "100."

Before the eating could begin, we all counted each row together by tens to reach the day's big number, then bagged our individual items up. Some of the kids were eager to start eating all one hundred items, but even more kept their bags untouched throughout the day, just for the satisfaction of looking at all one hundred of those things.

The One Hundredth Day of School

Math Buddies

• ◦ • ◦ •

Mentoring is a brain to pick, an ear to listen, and a push in the right direction.

John Crosby

Reading Buddies came to be a popular idea in the 1980s. The notion was that two teachers on different grade levels would arrange to get their classes together on a regular schedule. Each older student would be paired with a younger child, and either the older student would read a book to the younger one, or the younger would read to the older one, or both would take turns reading. The older students had the benefit of being "the big kid," a mentor, helping the younger children with their reading skills in a one-on-one setting. The younger child got the full and undivided attention of an older student, who praised her or him for sounding words out correctly, and helped on reading the difficult parts of the story. It was a win-win situation. In a debriefing in their classroom after their sessions, the older children would often talk about how they'd been able to help another child read and it felt good to do that. The younger children enjoyed their time with their "buddies," and often developed a mentor-mentee relationship with them.

As a second grade teacher, I began to wonder if a math buddy relationship could be as valuable for students as was a reading buddy arrangement. I proposed to a teacher who taught fourth grade that I could plan a lesson in an area of basic math to teach a math concept and share it with her, or vice versa.

Choosing to put a two-year gap between the groups was intentional. With only a one-year gap, some students may be too close in age to a buddy and the older student could have less credibility with the younger one. Two years is close enough the kids can still relate to each other, but the older one is viewed as more knowledgeable by the younger one. Three years – nope – too much distance in terms of thinking skills. Little kids are viewed as pests by the older ones.

The other teacher and I split our classes in half; she sent half her fourth graders to me and I sent half my second graders to her. In advance, we made pairings of the kids. We arranged it so the students going to the other class were each teacher's most able students, and each teacher kept in her own room kids who might need some additional help. We each taught the same lesson in our two different classrooms, and got together later to discuss how things went. We set it up as a weekly encounter for math, but we also occasionally ventured into science concepts and experiments.

One of my favorite lessons the Math Buddies did was to play a game called "Circles and Stars." I'm not sure where this game came from, but it's been around a while because I began playing it in 1993, and I still see references to it on the Internet. I like it because it benefits, on different levels, both the second graders and the fourth graders.

We began by making our scorekeeping book. The directions for making the book are in the Appendix. The book is not an essential part of this lesson, but it is fun to make, and it's a compact, handy tool for keeping score. Counting the front and back cover and without tearing any more folds (you don't want to do that or the whole thing falls apart), the book measures 3" x 4½" and has eight page surfaces. Have your students make a simple title on the front cover and write their name (e.g. By Sandy). Then number the remaining seven pages, including the back cover, with a small number in an upper corner of each page.

Directions to play "Circles and Stars":

- Each pair of students has one die.
- One student rolls the die and makes good sized circles on page one of his or her book to equal the number rolled.
- The other student rolls and does the same thing in his or her book.
- Back to the first student who rolls the die again. This time the student makes stars to equal the number on the die in *each* circle on page one. For instance, if this child has three circles and rolls a two on the second roll, there will be two stars in each one of the three circles for a total of six.
- This student writes the multiplication equation shown by the circles and stars (3 x 2 = 6) somewhere on page one.
- The other student rolls and does the same. Students compare their totals and see whose is larger. This is the winner of this round.
- Continue playing until all seven pages are complete.

Clearly a child doesn't have to be able to make a star to play this. You can use dots in the circle, or show children how to make a simple star * and leave it up to them about how they want to do it.

This game is an excellent introduction to repeated addition and, therefore, to multiplication for the second graders. Students can and did play it at home, and parents welcomed the chance to do this fun activity to help their student learn some times tables.

But wait, there's more! And this is why it was such a good Math Buddy activity. While the students were playing their rounds, I was making a chart on a big piece of bulletin board paper hanging at the front of the room. On the left side of the chart I wrote the numerals 1-18, one below the other. In the middle of the chart I wrote 19-36, also one below the other. As each team finished seven rounds, I asked them to come up to the chart paper with their score books and I recorded with tally marks every total on each player's book pages beside the appropriate number. If we had time, we could take a look at these results altogether, but even more valuable is the chance to send the chart back to the fourth graders' classroom for some in-depth analysis of why the scores fall out as they do.

There will be large numbers of scores of twelve. How did that happen? Answer: The die rolls can make 2 x 6, 6 x 2, 3 x 4 and 4 x 3. We also have large numbers of scores of six – 2 x 3, 3 x 2, 1 x 6, 6 x 1. Why do we have some numbers that are seldom or never rolled? Here's a good chance to identify some prime numbers (numbers that have only themselves and one as factors) and talk about them.

The second graders get value from this activity and, on an entirely different level, the fourth graders do too. Additionally, the fourth grade teacher reported to me her struggling fourth graders benefitted from this graphic way of looking at multiplication, maybe filling in a gap in their math understanding that no one ever knew was there. Even with this very logical demonstration of multiplication there will be fourth graders who don't know their times tables by heart. In doing this buddy activity, I could see the necessity of everyone having to master their multiplication facts and not always treating multiplication as repeated addition.

One year the fourth grade teacher and I decided to collect coins for a local charity. Students were asked to put only pennies, nickels, dimes, and quarters into a container in each of our classrooms if they wanted to donate. After a few weeks, each Math Buddy group got together and the buddies counted a pile of coins together. Handling and counting the different assortments of coins was great practice for my students, and the fourth graders benefitted from addition of series of numbers and work with multiplication to get totals. No calculators allowed!

At another session the Math Buddies worked with pattern blocks. The challenge for the Buddies was to use wooden pattern blocks to make as many different triangles as they possibly could, then glue down the paper representatives of the shapes. The fourth grade teacher made a poster of the results to display in her classroom. She arranged thirty-eight different triangles the Buddies had produced so they formed a large triangle and she titled it with this riddle – "Thirty-eight triangles are just fine. But can you find number thirty-nine?" Of course, the thirty-ninth triangle was the one formed by all the other triangles together.

We surveyed the fourth graders at the end of one of our years about their Math Buddy encounters. Most of their comments were very positive, but several of the fourth graders said they felt the activities were too easy for them. Clearly, more thought would be needed on the part of the teachers to give both levels of students a challenge every time we met, but we also felt that overall the experience had been useful for our classes.

18

The Value of Rotting Pumpkins

· · ● · ·

You never want to get into a plane where the pilot learned to fly from worksheets.

Justin Tarte

When I made the move from teaching first grade to teaching second grade, it was a profound experience for me. Second grade children could read independently. They could understand and follow written directions, and could express themselves in writing. They could work independently for more than twenty minutes at a time, and they were able to demonstrate their mastery of many social skills they had practiced in their earlier school years.

No matter what grade I taught, though, I felt my students should be exposed to real-life problems and situations in their learning experiences, and it was to serve this end that we watched a pumpkin rot. I had always used our Halloween pumpkin to teach and reinforce several academic lessons. We voted and tallied the score on how we wanted each part of the pumpkin's face to look: eyes, nose, and mouth. We carved the pieces out and handled and examined and commented upon them together. We all enjoyed the sensation of sticking our hands into the pumpkin's gooey insides, although some more than others. We collected, cleaned, and counted all the seeds and, of course, we roasted and ate the seeds together.

One year, it dawned on me it might be very interesting to see what happened when a pumpkin was left to rot. To facilitate our experiment, I put a nice layer of soil in a large terrarium and brought it to school. After Halloween, we placed the pumpkin into the terrarium, and I sealed the top tightly with plastic wrap. We discussed what might happen next, and I had each student illustrate how the pumpkin looked at that moment and write a speculation in a writing journal about what might occur as the pumpkin rotted. Nobody, including me, really knew what was going to happen, other than we said it would rot. So we watched.

After about a week the pumpkin began to sag in on itself. We continued to illustrate what we saw, revisiting and recording our observations every couple of weeks. The transition was fascinating, from sagging, to a growth of white fuzzy mold, to a change to black mold - all accompanied by a slow drooping of the pumpkin onto the surface of the soil. Some people might have felt it was gross but my students all seemed to find it interesting. The entire process took several months and, at the end, the only visible sign that something had been in the terrarium was the pumpkin's stem. Every other part of it had decomposed into the earth.

What an excellent opportunity for discussing where the pumpkin went and what purpose it might serve now. It led me to wonder aloud to my class about what would happen if we were to bury some things in the dirt of the terrarium and watch to see what would happen to them too. Would any item decompose and turn back into soil? The idea was met with much enthusiasm, and we talked about what we might want to bury. In the end, we buried a Styrofoam cup, a page from a newspaper, a banana peel, a plastic water bottle, and a rock. And then we left it all for time and the earth to do whatever they were going to do.

We knew the process would take time, and we resisted digging into the dirt to see what was happening. That wasn't easy. After a period of two months, we took a trowel and dug in, and this was what we found: the banana peel was gone except for a tiny bit of the stem; the newspaper page had disintegrated into an unreadable, soggy mass; and the rock looked just as it had when we buried it in the earth. As for the plastic water bottle and the Styrofoam cup? Other than being dirty, they appeared exactly as they had at the beginning of the experiment and, with a wash, could have gone on doing the function for which they were first invented. An interesting discussion ensued. I can only hope my students have kept the lesson of the items in our world that are *not* biodegradable with them to this day, and it affected their future behavior as consumers and disposers of unwanted items.

Several years later, I planned the pumpkin experiment with a group of fourth graders. I set up the terrarium with a good layer of dirt and we placed the pumpkin within. I sealed and taped it over tightly with plastic wrap and we began our observation. After a few days, the parent of one of my students contacted me. She was quite concerned about the possible effects to her child's health of having the pumpkin rotting in our classroom. She was very insistent I end the experiment as soon as possible, and threatened to take her complaint to my principal. By great good luck, I had a teacher friend whose husband was a microbiologist. He had spoken to my class a few days before about his job. I called him and asked a big favor. Would he be willing to talk to this mother, and assure her the pumpkin posed no danger? Bless his heart, he called her up at home, and convinced her we would all survive the rotting pumpkin experiment.

After three years in second grade, I moved on to third. Part of my third graders' curriculum was a study of nutrition in their science unit. I remembered when my middle son studied this topic, and would sort our groceries in the cart according to their food groups. The students in my class learned the food groups also. Then I introduced my class to the daily food pyramid and we created a model of it on the whiteboard. The pyramid at that time recommended five-seven servings of fruits and vegetables, three-five servings of cereals, breads, potatoes, rice and pasta, three servings of milk, yogurts, and cheeses, two servings of meats, poultry, cheeses, eggs, and, at the top, one-two servings of fatty foods and foods with sugar per day. In order to get a notion of what my students were actually eating, I went around the classroom, listing on the board what one child had had for breakfast that day, another child's midmorning snack, another's lunch, another's after school snack, and another's evening meal.

We then classified those actual foods according to the category they fit into on the pyramid, and the number of servings the students had reported in each category. I drew the pyramid (which was now nowhere near a pyramid!) in the proportions the students' servings suggested. The results were staggering. The pyramid base for fruits and vegetables was still the largest, and close to the same in numbers of servings, but it was composed almost entirely of fruits. The section for cereals, breads, etc. was as large as the base. The dairy and meat sections were fairly close to the recommended amounts. The very worrisome part was the top: it should have been smallest of all, but instead was near the size of the base. My students were eating *a lot* of fatty foods and sugars.

I wasn't sure how far we could go with this study, but I did two more things. I reported the results in my next newsletter to parents, and I decreed that my students needed to make sure that sugars (including sucrose and fructose) were not listed among the first three ingredients of the daily snack they brought to school. Parents proved to be very supportive and my class, as only third graders know how to do, rapidly came to become strict monitors of their own and other's eating habits. Hooray! I wonder if that lesson stuck with those kids beyond that year. I know they did get to be very skilled at reading food labels.

Another good lesson happened one day with no plan from me. I had arranged for a visit to my classroom of a local woman who was a member of the Cherokee tribe. She came dressed in a full tribal costume, and told the children about the significance and symbolism of the clothes she was wearing, and also shared some tribal legends. As her time with us grew near an end, she explained she needed to leave school to go to her job, and she began shedding her costume. Underneath she was dressed in western-style business clothes and, by the time her costume and props were packed away, she looked like a modern 20th century woman.

I told her later how valuable I thought it was for my students to see her emerge in her business clothes, how, in a symbolic way, this helped them to see Native Americans are a part of our larger society, but their culture endures and continues to be important to them. The valuable lesson the speaker taught my students was unintended on her part, but we both agreed that it was a perfect way to end her visit with us.

Teachable Moments

• · ● · •

Students will ask some great questions that might not be on topic. Don't forfeit a "teachable moment" for the sake of your lesson plan.

Danny Steele

Teachable Moments - I watched for them every day in my life as a teacher. Their appearance could wreak havoc with my plans for the day, but their value was not to be denied. One of my favorites occurred early in one school year after I had taken a weekend trip with my husband to Las Vegas. I am not any kind of a gambler but, on that trip, I sat down at the nickel slots, and entertained myself for the better part of an hour with $20. It was a fruitful hour, and, at one point, I hit the jackpot. Lights flashed and bells rang as 1,000 nickels poured into my slot machine's tray. Of course, 1,000 nickels isn't much money, but it sounds like a lot.

On Monday, I reported on my weekend trip to my class. I told them I had been a big winner, and of course they demanded to know what I'd won. I said, "I won 1,000… (long pause as their eyes grew big)… nickels!" Now, to third graders, 1,000 of *anything* still sounds like a bunch of money and they instantly wanted to know how much that was. We had been beginning to work on division in math, so I asked my students to figure out just how much money had poured out of the slot machine. We had not learned anything at this point about applying an algorithm to division, so the kids were left with using reasoning skills and manipulatives to work through the problem. Lots of discussion ensued as they worked individually and with each other to think about my challenge. It wasn't very long before several someones announced that my winnings totaled $50. We talked about the various methods they had employed to find the answer, and for me, this is the best part of a teachable moment - having the whole class engaged and interested, and being able to see where my students are in their thinking. The answer itself wasn't nearly as important as the processes students used to get there.

I always kept my eyes peeled for things to contribute to my lessons at school – abandoned birds' nests, garage sale bargains, interesting shells and rocks, etc. For many years a weathered animal skull sat in my science center, a stimulus for curiosity and detailed investigation.

One summer while my family was traveling in Montana, we visited the Range Rider's Museum in Miles City. The museum offered, for fifty cents each, cut and polished Montana moss agates in many beautiful colors and patterns. Moss agates are stones commonly found near the Yellowstone River. On the outside they are a rough rock, but when sliced into slabs and polished, they reveal beautiful black, gray and orange patterns that resemble mountains, water, animals, and landscapes, each one unique and unpredictable. I had lived in this part of Montana as a child, and remembered my fascination with polished agates. I asked the sales clerk if she might have twenty-seven of these stones I could buy to give to my third grade class in Florida when the school year began. She didn't have that many in stock, but said she could get that amount and mail them to me. I paid her in advance for the agates and for her estimation of the shipping charge.

When the school year started, the agates had not yet reached me. I was eager for their arrival, but weeks passed and I began to suspect I had been suckered. As more weeks went by, I was sure of it. Then, one day, I received a box from the museum. I opened it to find a cardboard cigar box, tightly packed, full of polished agates, each one carefully wrapped in a Kleenex tissue. They were beautiful, each one with its own individual design and no two the same. The next day, before my third grade students came into the classroom, I lay one tissue-wrapped agate on each child's desk. There were enough to go around with a few extras.

When the children came into the classroom, I explained about my summer trip to the museum, and told them what an agate was. They unwrapped their tissue packages, and we marveled at all the different colors and designs in the stones. I then said I realized, because we had so many different designs and colors, they might find themselves comparing their agate with others, and may want to make a trade. I said I didn't really mind that, but I wanted us to do it and be done with it. At my signal, they would have two minutes on the classroom clock to do any trading they wanted, and then it would be over and finished. What they would keep was what they would have at the end of the time.

The two minutes began, and I watched a fascinating demonstration of social behavior unfold before my eyes. Some of the children instantly began darting around the room, seeking to trade, not just once, but two, three, and four times, seemingly caught up in trading just for the sake of doing it, without much thought to which agate they really wanted to keep. Others were more reluctant until they saw what someone else had and, after some consideration, agreed to trade. Other children seemed to be satisfied with what they had at the onset, stayed at their seat and refused anyone else's offer. By the end of the two minutes, I called "Time!" and it was over. The agates were tucked away until they went home at the end of the day. This way of giving children a degree of control over their choices and responsibility for the outcome worked well, and I used a variation of it many times in my teacher life.

In terms of teachable moments, this experience with the agates was one for me. As the school year progressed, I often reflected on the implications of what I saw that day. Was I being given a glimpse of developing personalities, from the person who is never quite content with his or her lot in life, and who constantly seeks something else, to the thoughtful person who considers what he or she desires, and then strives for it, to the person who accepts whatever life throws his or her way? An interesting thought. I often wish I had had the chance to know those children as adults, just to see if that third grade behavior was, indeed, a foreshadowing of my students' future personalities.

Another time I was observing a second grade teacher teaching a math lesson. In the midst of her lesson, the class' monarch butterfly began to emerge from its cocoon. This excellent teacher did not miss a beat. She paused her lesson, and every child watched in awe as the miraculous moment unfolded. They all discussed what was happening as it occurred, and the transition from math to science was seamless. That's an excellent example of a teacher making use of a teachable moment.

As grade level curriculum expectations have become more and more rigid, the opportunities for a teacher to take advantage of a teachable moment shrink dramatically. I was appalled one day to see a quote by a principal of a local school:

"When I can walk down the hall of a grade level at my school and hear the exact same lesson and words coming from each room, I will know my teachers are doing their jobs well," he said.

No teachable moments permitted there, just strict adherence to a preset timetable and rigid formulaic teaching.

A skilled teacher watches for those opportunities when she or he can seize upon ordinary events, unexpected student questions, or serendipitous moments to extend a lesson or impart knowledge. You never know when a teachable moment will pop up, but you want to always be ready.

Parent/Teacher Relations

At the end of the day, the most overwhelming key to a child's success is the positive involvement of parents.

Jane D. Hull

A s a teacher, you are in a partnership with the parents of each child in your class. It's a commitment from parent and teacher to work together to achieve what you both want for your student – the best possible chance for a fruitful learning experience and cooperation between the two of you that is in the best interest of the child you are sharing this year.

Home visits

As I've discussed earlier, there is nothing like an informal home visit to help you gain understanding and empathy about the life your student leads out of school. As valuable as it is, this is not an easy event for parents and teachers to schedule, and I feel I was lucky to be able to do it for the years I did. Generally, if this can't be arranged, your parent/teacher contacts will be at school with a formal conference, or through a Meet-the-Teacher night early in the school year.

Meet-the-Teacher

Meet the Teacher night involves giving parents a brief opportunity to interact with their child's teacher in his or her classroom. For my kindergartners and first graders, we prepared for this evening event by tracing each child's body onto white bulletin board paper. Students would then color on their clothes and features to make a large paper person who looked "just like them." I would cut these out, or enlist a volunteer to do it.

On Meet-the-Teacher night, I arranged each of the paper people at the owner's desk, hands neatly folded in front of them. The kids were excited their parents got to see the person they made sitting at their own desk, and the parents enjoyed taking the project home. I frequently saw these characters proudly displayed when I made the home visit later in the year. After arranging the paper people at their desks, I could never resist savoring a moment, appreciating all the quiet, well-behaved children populating my classroom.

Let's take a moment here to recognize the value of volunteers and teacher assistants. These selfless individuals, working for free in the case of volunteers, and low pay in the case of teacher assistants, can be the backbone of a classroom, handling jobs such as cutting out paper people, or working with small groups who need extra help, or accompanying a class on field trips. If you are lucky enough to have a volunteer or assistant, make sure you take the time to plan for them to be in your classroom. I know that's not always easy, but they are giving you their valuable time and it should be acknowledged. In the case of a volunteer, it may take a while to assess that person's talents and decide how you can best use him or her. But the planning can pay off by freeing you from routine classroom chores. Sometimes a volunteer just doesn't work out, either because of lack of skills or because his or her reasons for coming into your classroom are not so much about being helpful to you, as about being around his or her child. Such a situation calls for thoughtful tact. Mostly, volunteers are a wonderful addition to a classroom. I was pleased to have them be a part of the educational experience of my students and always tried to show them my appreciation and gratitude.

Meet-the-Teacher night is a chance for teachers to go over the curriculum, to discuss homework procedures, and to give out general information. It is not a chance for parent conferences. As a parent, I was happy at those times to see my child's classroom, to be formally introduced to the teacher, and to try to gain a sense of what my child would be studying over the course of the year. As a teacher, you will want parents to leave this night feeling that you will be a positive partner with them in their child's education this year. If a parent wishes to have a conference, schedule it for another day.

One thing I've heard teachers say on Meet-the-Teacher Night that tickles my funny bone, both as a parent and a teacher –

"If you promise not to believe half the things your child says happen at school, I promise not to believe half the things he says happen at home."

Inviting Parents to Participate in School

It's good for parents to see their children in school, to get a feel for how they interact with other children in class, and to have some exposure to the lessons the class is learning. On several occasions, I invited parents to stay with us after a program or to come in for a portion of the day and do a math lesson with us. As I remarked to parents in inviting them to school, "This is your chance to find out what your child really means when you say, 'What did you do at school today?' and your child says, 'Nothing.'"

As I used more and more math manipulative materials and taught using more modern math terminology ("regrouping" instead of "borrowing" or "trading," for instance), I felt it important for parents to see this in person. On one occasion, my second graders spent an entire afternoon in their math centers with about twelve parents moving through the centers with their own child. The groups rotated through four activities – making a fraction kit (See the Appendix for directions), playing the game Race to One Hundred with a calculator (See the Appendix), a pattern block lesson, and doing a worksheet.

After three rotations I asked the worksheet groups which they preferred - hands-on lessons or paper-and-pencil lessons. The hands-on lessons won by a landslide, from both parents and kids. That day I had a chance to talk with a few of the parents about my hope that the math manipulative materials would continue to get used when this class reached third grade. It never hurts to enlist a little parent pressure when you want to influence good practices.

Conferences

Parent-Teacher Conferences

Sometimes conferences are part of the school routine – a school-wide conference day that gives you the chance to meet parents one-on-one, to talk about student progress, and have a comfortable sense of what their child's classroom life is like.

At other times, though, you have a need to meet with parents to resolve a problem a student is experiencing in the classroom. This can be initiated by either you or the parent. Here are a few tips to help these face-to-face meetings go well:

- If you are initiating a conference because of difficulty a student is having in your class, document the classroom incidents or work products that concern you before you schedule the conference. It takes very little time to jot the date and a short note for yourself, and to save work products in a folder.

- It may be appropriate to include the student as a member of the conference team. You and the parent can decide if this would be helpful. Even if you don't, you want the student to know you and his or her parents are on the same page and have the same goals, and you will be keeping in close touch with each other.

+ Before you ever begin a parent conference, mentally prepare yourself with positive assumptions about how the meeting will go.

+ Start the meeting with a sincere positive comment about your student. Be prepared to tell the parent where his or her child is excelling, and also where the student needs help.

+ The best advice I can give you when you have a parent conference is listen, listen, listen. You will be tempted to jump right in to give advice, to propose plans, to prove your competence as an educator. This will all fall on deaf ears if you have not first truly listened with an open heart and mind to what this child's parent has to say.

+ Your next step is to establish a sense of partnership. Begin with the certain notion that you both want what is best for the child. This is something you can agree on, right from the start.

+ Work together to find a solution. You may decide to communicate more regularly; the parent may agree to more closely monitor homework. Whatever you decide, state it clearly and establish you are both buying into this solution.

+ Following the conference, document what was discussed and the course of action you and the parent agreed upon, while it is still fresh in your mind.

Be aware you are not going to please every parent all of the time. There will be the parent who pressures you to make a grade an A instead of a B, or the parent who adamantly refuses to believe his or her child could have kicked, cheated, or misbehaved in any way. Keep your cool and always remember, bottom line, both you and the parent want to do what's best for the student.

No matter how good a teacher you are, you will not be universally liked by every parent you encounter. As every teacher does, I had some experiences with parents who were unhappy with me. One year, I was assigned front hall duty in the morning before school. Parents were required to sign in at the office before going into any classroom, a common safety practice in all schools. A parent walked past me one day with a child in tow, and I told him he would have to check into the office first. He was in a hurry and argued he couldn't wait to do the office check-in. I insisted, he argued. I told him it was a safety measure and would only take a minute. Finally, he angrily went into the office, signed in, and brushed past me to escort his child. A few minutes later he strode past me on the way out, still angry, and saying something about how he would have my job. Not a great start to the day, for either one of us, and not great for his child either. I reported what had happened to the office staff to be on the safe side.

My friend, Joanne McCarthy, told me the story about how one day, after her students had gone home, the school secretary called her on the intercom to come to the office to take a phone call. When she arrived at the office, the secretary mouthed to her that an irate parent was on the line. Joanne identified herself to the parent and asked how she could help. Without even identifying herself, the parent on the phone began shouting, "How dare you teach sex education to my son! I did not give you my permission! That is a parent's responsibility and, furthermore, he's way too young to be taught about sex!"

Joanne was bewildered and befuddled and told the mother she had no idea what she was talking about. She had taught no such lesson. "Well," said the mother, "my son came home from school today and told me you had showed the class a movie in sex." Joanne was hard pressed to contain her laughter when she told the mother the class had watched a movie that day about *insects*. They shared a good laugh and the mother apologized.

Another time, a parent called me on the last teacher workday of the school year. Her child had received a barely less-than-perfect assessment on his end-of-year report in the gifted program. I listened, and as per my earlier advice to you, listened some more as this mother set out all the reasons she felt her child should have had perfect numbers on the assessment. After about ten minutes, I asked her to hold on a minute while I went to our files and took out the form we were discussing. The form had been on my desk all along, but I needed a second to decompress. I lay the phone down gently, bent down to the floor, and very quietly pounded my hands on the carpet for a few seconds. Then I stood up and was able to calmly tell the mom that the scores on the assessment had been carefully considered during the grading process; that they accurately reflected her child's performance, and they would not be changed.

If you are ever faced at your classroom door with an angry parent, make an appointment for a conference. Don't try to solve the problem with a classroom full of students waiting for you. Ask a principal, counselor, or colleague to sit in on a conference with you if you are the least bit uncomfortable or feel your safety may be threatened.

Student-led Conferences

This is an excellent way to give children ownership of their learning. One year, I was visiting at a school on the day when each member of a class of fourth graders was conducting his/her own parent-teacher-student conference. Students had prepared in advance to showcase for their parents the work they had been doing. They were each also going over an assessment on which both the student and the teacher had separately evaluated student performance. It was interesting to notice that students frequently had given themselves lower scores than had their teacher on their assessments. The teacher told me later this was not unusual - that, given the chance to grade themselves, students often held themselves to very high standards. The parent, the teacher, and the student conferred during this conference. I could see it was a satisfying, productive experience for everyone involved.

Home-School Communication

Class newsletters, a quick response to parent notes or emails, and some routine for weekly feedback on student performance are all good home/school communication tools. Class newsletters can be a weekly or monthly event. They can include news of upcoming field trips or programs, a list of class needs (hand sanitizer or tissues), student essays, whatever you feel is important to pass along. Don't tie yourself up in knots to do an elaborate newsletter, though. It can consume a lot of your time. Asking students to write about things that have happened in the classroom is a good writing exercise for them and a good communication tool for you to include in a newsletter.

It is always important to answer parent emails in a timely manner, but don't sacrifice instructional time to do this unless it's an emergency. The instructional time you have with your students is limited and valuable and should always be a priority.

If you need additional information about parent conferences, the internet has some good advice. Check out these sites: www.nea.org, kidshealth.org, www.care.com, and turnitin.com. And, if you need an encouraging laugh, the internet can also offer you some lighthearted humor on the topic too!

Theodore Seuss Geisel
and Shel Silverstein

· · • · ·

Picking five favorite books is like picking the five body parts you'd most like not to lose.

Neil Gaiman

Theodore Geisel, or Dr. Seuss, as he is known by millions of children, is one of my favorite children's book authors. From my own earliest years, around age three, I was captivated by his stories in verse and his wild illustrations. His birthday is March 2 and, as a teacher, I have celebrated it year after year with my students. Whether they were kindergartners, first graders, or second graders, we always wrote happy birthday letters to Dr. Seuss. We also cooked green eggs and ham (See the Appendix for the recipe) and read and talked about his books. A few years into our letter writing to Dr. Seuss, my students began to receive answers from him. At first, they were obviously pre-printed, with the famous Cat in the Hat on one side of the page and a message from Dr. Seuss on the other side. After a few years the letters became more personal, as you can see from this one.

One
Very Special
Green Egg
for
my
Very Special
friends
at
Conway!

Dr. Seuss

The exchange of letters went on for several years with different groups of my students. And then one day, September 24th of 1991, our media specialist showed up at the door of my second grade classroom. She pulled me aside and said, "I know you were so fond of Dr. Seuss, and I felt I should come down to tell you I've just heard he has died."

I couldn't have been more devastated had it been a member of my own family. I mourned for days.

Later that year my middle son, Patrick, was assigned to give the benediction at his senior class Baccalaureate ceremony. We both searched and searched for an appropriate quote to mark his classmates' graduation from high school. Patrick was not at all comfortable with this public speaking chore, and could not find words he wanted to say. Eventually we turned to his and my favorite author, Dr. Seuss. At the ceremony Patrick explained he would be quoting from Dr. Seuss' words, and he read the ending verses from Dr. Seuss' book, *Oh, the Places You'll Go!*, finishing by telling his graduating classmates, "Today is your day! Your mountain is waiting. So…get on your way!" (From *Oh, the Places You'll Go* by Dr. Seuss)

A few weeks later, I wrote a letter to Audrey Geisel, Theodore Geisel's wife. I told her about my own longstanding fan relationship with her husband and I also recounted what Patrick had done for the Baccalaureate ceremony. She answered with a touching personal note, thanking me for sharing some of my Dr. Seuss memories. The most poignant part of her letter, though, was the picture of the Cat on the side of the notepaper. Dr. Seuss' Cat had been the smiling one we all know so well. Audrey Geisel's letter had the same Cat but his expression was sad, with tears running down his face, perfectly expressing the grief so many people were experiencing at the loss of this beloved storyteller and artist.

January 9, 1992

Dear Colleen:

Thank you so much for
your kind letter and
for all the wonderful
things you remember
about Dr. Seuss. You
and your family shared
some wonderful memories
of his work and his
books.

I appreciate your
relating how Patrick
chose some lines from
Oh, The Places You'll
Go for his high school
Baccalaureate ceremony.

With very best wishes
to all of you!

Audrey S. Geisel

Another favorite poet/author of my students, no matter what their grade level, was Shel Silverstein. His funny, and often profound, poems rollicked across all sorts of topics with exaggerations, personifications, alliteration, interesting rhythms, and original illustrations by the poet.

For one of my lessons, I asked my second grade students to listen as I read Silverstein's "The Crocodile's Toothache." This poem tells the story of a crocodile's visit to a dentist. The dentist climbs right into the crocodile's mouth, pulling teeth right and left, laughing "What's one crocodile's tooth, more or less?" Suddenly the crocodile's jaws go *snap* and the dentist is nowhere to be seen. The poem ends, "But what's one dentist, more or less?"

I read in a monotone, running lines together and ignoring all the punctuation. When I finished, I asked for comments and I got an earful. My students said I needed to be reading with a lot more expression, and I should be paying attention to all of the periods, commas and question marks. I asked, "Do you think you can do it better?" They responded with lots of "Yeses!" I asked for volunteers who would like to read the poem aloud to the rest of us in the way they thought it should be read. Several of the kids wanted to come up and try it. After each one read, we discussed the improvements they had made over my earlier reading and came up with suggestions that would make it even better. Two or three students read the poem to their classmates. When they finished, I told them I had a recording of someone else reading the poem and wanted to know how they liked that version. What I didn't reveal was that my recording was Shel Silverstein himself.

Silverstein read as no one else has ever read that poem. He shrieked, and shouted, lowered his voice at times and raised it at others, ran on lines and ignored a lot of the same punctuation marks as I had. When the recording finished I asked, "What do you think about that?"

The kids did not mince words. Almost no one liked the way the poem was read this time. They were critical of just about everything, and we had a lively discussion about why anyone would have read this poem in that way. And then, I told them who had been reading. What a great opportunity for more lively discussion about whether the author of a poem has ownership of the way it's presented to an audience. Shel Silverstein very much had led us to an even greater appreciation of poetry and poets that day.

Shel Silverstein continued to be a favorite poet for my students, no matter what grade level I taught. In 1978, Congress passed legislation to officially decree the first Sunday after Labor Day would be Grandparents Day in the United States. I didn't realize this day had been made a part of the calendar until several years later but, in the meantime, I'd taken it upon myself to celebrate Grandparents Day in my classroom near the end of each school year. We sent an RSVP invitation to the day for grandparents and senior citizen friends. I arranged for older friends of mine to attend and stand in with any child who didn't have a grown-up to come for them. I asked my students to singly or with a partner of their choice select a poem to memorize or plan a joke to tell from the many resources in our classroom.

It was no surprise to me that Silverstein's *A Light in the Attic* and *Where the Sidewalk Ends* became the students' go-to books for their poetry to perform for their grandparents and senior citizen friends. As the grandparents arrived, I had each student formally introduce his or her guest to me. We served our guests punch and cookies, and then the show began. Students had all made a poster to illustrate their poem and had planned for their props, as needed. Alone or in pairs, students came to the front of the classroom to perform. I made sure I gave very little input other than facilitating where necessary. As always, my students rose to the occasion, and surprised and delighted me with their enterprise and cuteness. Of course, the grandparents agreed wholeheartedly with my evaluation.

Was that done "just for fun?" Certainly not. Memorizing a poem is a good thing to learn to do. Learning to introduce adults to each other is a commendable social skill. Having control over the work you memorize lets you pick what you're comfortable with. Doing a show in the classroom for grandparents is about as low threat as any public performance can be, and helps you to gain confidence for future performances. And finally, I am very much aware, when you ask an elementary-aged kid his or her most memorable moment in school, it's never, "I loved the way my teacher taught me multiplication." It will always be more along the lines of, "That program we did for our grandparents when I was in third grade is what I remember best."

I guess it's the same for teachers too. My friend, Marsha Ranieri, who taught second grade in North Syracuse, New York, for many years, recalls one of her favorite memories from her teaching career was when she put on plays with her classes at the end of the school year. It was a collaborative effort. Parents were involved in the making of costumes, creating sets, and designing and publishing the program. The music teacher was invaluable when dealing with logistics of providing music and helping children learn songs, and choreographing the dance steps. The art teacher worked cooperatively with parents providing input, suggestions, and materials needed to make the sets.

When you engage students in a performance or in reciting lines from a favorite poet or writer, have fun with it. You will often see children rise to a level you didn't realize they had in them, and you will almost always be astonished with watching the play come off without a hitch!

Interacting with School Administrators

• • • • •

The principal can either extinguish a flame of positivity or ignite a flame of hope.

Dr. Marcus Jackson

For me, and I suspect for all teachers, intricately interwoven with the words "school administrators" and "department heads" is the word "meetings." This begins from the very first day we reenter the school building after summer vacation. Generally, the first day of pre-planning will be a day-long meeting about procedures, routines, schedules, rules, and plans for future meetings. Sometimes there will be a "mixer," designed to help staff members get to know each other.

As much as I could recognize the need for all the instructional staff to come together for some period of time, I was impatient, restless, and excited to get into my classroom - to set up desks, inventory textbooks, create bulletin boards, plan lessons - in short, to get ready to teach. Inevitably, those first day meetings went on far longer than I wanted them to, and I often couldn't discern a good purpose for them. One of the worst was a year when the school system had a new superintendent. For the entirety of one preplanning workday, all the teachers in the county were bused to a downtown auditorium for a mass introduction, multiple speeches, and a "pep" rally. What a massive waste of time!!

If I could have been in charge of those first day meetings, I would have made sure it lasted no more than a half-day and, in truth, I did have the pleasure of working for a few principals who did exactly that. However, over my working years with eighteen different principals, short, succinct, well-organized meetings were a rarity. If, after, more than thirty years, I didn't have the power to reduce the number of meetings or to have a major impact on how a school was managed, I'm thinking you may not either. In the best of all possible education worlds, though, here are a few observations I have regarding the people who are in charge in schools:

- A good school administrator should, first and foremost, have real classroom teaching experience. Not one or two years of working as a classroom teacher but, in my view, at least five years and, preferably, over more than one grade level. Just as I feel you should not be in the classroom if you don't like kids, I also strongly feel you should not be a principal if you are not fond of children. The story of *Matilda* by Roald Dahl comes to mind and; if you want a terrible example of a principal, check it out.

- Even though classroom teachers are isolated in their own classrooms, we should grab every chance to communicate with each other. I know – I can hear you saying you don't have time to do your own planning, much less to coordinate with someone else. A good administrator should help with that. I am remembering a principal who somehow worked it out that, for a portion of one day each year, teachers had a chance to meet and have a targeted discussion with the teachers on either side of the grade level in which they worked. This same principal arranged to make it possible for teachers to spend some time observing in another classroom on their grade level.

Her efforts paid off in helping all of us to better coordinate our curricula, and to send our students on to the next grade as well prepared as possible.

- My very best administrators were supportive of their teachers. If I had a parent problem, they would back me up, possibly meeting with me and the parent together, always taking the approach that I was a professional and knew what I was doing. If one of my students' parents went to my principal with a problem in my classroom, a good principal would talk to me after the meeting and before making any final decision about resolving the issue. I know the job of principal is hard, a job I would never want to do, but it brings with it the responsibility to set a professional tone with parents and teachers, and to be competent enough to navigate the difficulties that can arise between them.

- My best principals were a visible presence in the hallways and classrooms of the school. Some of them made a point of greeting students at the front door of the school at the beginning of the school day, or wishing them good-bye as they left in the afternoon. Some made sure to be in the cafeteria at some point during lunchtime. I was comfortable with a principal dropping into my classroom unannounced, but some teachers find this intimidating; a good principal is sensitive to that possibility. Principals who spend a part of each day walking through the school's hallways will have a sense of how well the school is running. Unfortunately, in my experience, many of them were sequestered in their offices for the bulk of the school day. An entire day could pass without some of those principals once seeing the face of a live child. Or, even worse, seeing only the children who were sent to the office for misbehavior.

+ And, back to the subject of meetings. Good administrators recognize that meetings can be gobblers of important and limited minutes. They trust teachers to use their time wisely, and make every effort to give them more of it. On one occasion a colleague and I were attending an all-day downtown meeting. The speaker droned on and on, peppering her presentation with the word "like," something that was driving both my colleague and me crazy. During a restroom break, the two of us decided to tally her use of "like" in places where it didn't belong and, if the number reached fifty by lunchtime, we would treat ourselves to dessert. We became much more attentive to what was being said thereafter – or, at least, to that particular word, and we did get dessert.

My friend Mardi McMakin taught French and German at the high school and middle school level. One year, her assistant principal did her classroom observation. Later, he went over the observation and discussed the very positive evaluation he had made of her teaching her French class. Except, although he gave her kudos for speaking with students during the practice drill, he noted she had completely ignored three students. She reminded him that the school had an arrangement whereby several study hall students were assigned, due to space problems, to do study hall in various classrooms during class time, and that these three were busy doing their homework in her room. Somewhat sheepishly the administrator apologized, and corrected his mistake on her observation form.

When *you're* in Charge of Meetings

Of course, there will be times when *you* will have responsibility for holding and planning a meeting, such as a grade level meeting when you're grade chairperson, for instance. In that case:

- Be respectful of the value of your colleague's time.

- Plan the topic of the meeting in advance, stick to the topic, and keep control of the meeting.

- If another teacher begins talking about an issue that isn't of concern for the entire group, suggest who he or she can contact to talk about that and move on.

- Keep the meeting as short as possible.

- Remember, ending a meeting early will always earn you brownie points from teachers.

This topic of meetings reminds me of the occasion when I had an exchange teacher from Beijing, China. One day I was leaving our classroom to attend a teachers' meeting. My exchange teacher exclaimed, "Meetings, meetings, meetings. You are always going to meetings. In China we do not have to have so many meetings. They just tell us what to do and we do it!" I confess, I don't think I would be willing to give up all meetings to experience teaching life in Communist China.

Our Year-Round-School Adventure

. . ● . .

> The trouble with organizing a thing is that pretty soon
> folks get to paying more attention to the organization
> than to what they're organized for.
>
> Laura Ingalls Wilder

For a period in the early 1990s through 1997, Orange County Public Schools in Florida instituted year-round-schools in, at first all, and later, in just some of its elementary schools. Although the new program was sold to the public as an educational decision, its real purpose was to ease some serious classroom overcrowding.

Each of the six classroom teachers on my second grade level was placed into a "track," designated by various colors. I was on the yellow track and, as such, my school year began in mid-July. The last week of August, after twenty-five school days (5 weeks) in school, my students and I had a three-week break. We returned near the end of September, and were in school nine more weeks until we had a short break just before Thanksgiving. We came back in early December. On December 21st, we started a five week winter break. When we came back on January 24th we were in school again until mid-April. The next break lasted from April 15-May 11. This schedule continued until my students had completed the required 180 days of the school year, finally ending sometime in June. To say it was confusing is a gross understatement, not to mention a scheduling nightmare for the school officials in charge of creating the six tracks.

While my students were gone from "our" classroom, another group of third graders, the orange track, was using the space as their classroom. When we returned, those children moved into another vacated classroom, thus making it possible to use the space of only five classrooms for six classes of children.

The original plan was to have all of the classes rotating from classroom to classroom, a constantly moving cycle in the sixty-five schools in Orange County. Very early on, someone realized this was an even more chaotic plan than the wildly confusing schedule itself. The decision was made to designate only one track as the "rover," the class that would pack up and move to a vacated classroom multiple times over the course of the year.

The job as the rover was not a popular assignment, and it tended to fall on the newest and least experienced teacher on the grade level. In gratitude to that teacher, the rest of us knew we should make sure our classrooms were well prepared for the incoming group, maybe leaving a welcome card on the desks for her students, a candy bar treat on the teacher's desk, and trying to make the move as smooth for her as possible. It wasn't easy though, I'm sure, packing up lock, stock, and barrel several times over the course of the school year, and transporting everything to a new classroom. A real nightmare for the teacher, the students, and the custodial crew.

There were possible benefits I could see, though, in having the longer breaks throughout the school year and a shorter summer vacation. I expected students would retain more from grade to grade and wouldn't need as much review time when each school year started. The breaks meant families could take vacations at formerly impossible times of the year, and have a good down-time between each school period. Siblings in elementary school were placed on the same track so their schedules meshed, but middle schools and high schools continued to operate on a traditional schedule. At first, I found it disorienting to have a school vacation in September, just when my classes would ordinarily begin to be well-organized and running smoothly. I felt sort of like I was playing hooky when I was out in public. On the plus side, I could now take an autumn mountain vacation, and maybe see leaves change color (something I missed in Florida).

However, the entire experiment was chaotic and unsettling – for teachers, students, and parents. Several of the tracks had weird schedules, such as beginning a new school year in the hottest times of the summer, certainly not the best time to confine children in a classroom. Parents could request a track, but were not assured of getting their first choice, and there was much unrest because of that. After-school centers had to operate on a full schedule all year round. Our resource teachers - special education, gifted education, physical education, art and music - had to become year-round employees, whether they wanted to or not. The school cafeteria had to operate year-round, as did the janitorial staff and the bus drivers, greatly increasing costs to the county. Hoped-for academic benefits of students not having a long summer break were not realized.

Sometimes new and innovative ideas are a good thing. We should never be prematurely dismissive of them, and should always give them a chance to work. Whole language, new math, Common Core, all-day kindergarten, open-space classrooms, charter and magnet schools, were all someone's notion of education reforms which would be new and improved and would solve educational problems. For my colleagues and I, though, year-round-school felt like a bad idea, set up by administrators and/or politicians who had little to no knowledge of or concern for children's and families' developmental, economic, and social needs.

Real Life Social Studies

● ● ● ● ●

There's no place like home.

L. Frank Baum

As my teaching years passed at Conway Elementary, my student populations became more and more diverse. We were located in a rapidly growing and changing part of rapidly growing and changing Orlando and, to our majority white student body, were added more Black, Asian, and Latino children every year.

Because of our changing population, in 1991, I applied for, and was awarded a $3,200 grant from Orange County Schools for the purchase of geography and social studies materials for kindergarten through third grade students. I had a wonderful time asking my teacher colleagues, our Curriculum Resource teacher, and our media specialist what we could use, and spending every last bit of that money. I bought laminated desk maps, large wall maps, atlases, geography games, puzzles, children's books and magazines, and teacher resource books on the United States and many other countries.

I enjoyed weaving geography and social studies into our math, literature, and science lessons. My students wrote to pen pals in other states. For a few years, we wrote to students in Villeneuve-d'Ascq, France, where I had a teacher friend. Ghislaine was the mother of an exchange student who had lived with my family in the 1980s, and her students were near the same age as my third graders. We wrote in English to our French pen pals, and the students from Ghislaine's class at École René Clair wrote in French. At both ends, the teachers had some challenges in translating, but we enlisted help from dictionaries and people who spoke the language, and we exchanged tiny mementos, maps, information about our state of Florida and their region of France, and facts about our countries in focused communication the teacher and I planned.

One year, my Conway third graders participated in a competition to win a set of encyclopedia. For those of you who are not familiar with them, these sets were our Google before the age of Google. A set consisted of multiple volumes of alphabetized photos and information about every subject and topic one could imagine. We were the grand prize winners, and the members of my class quickly became eager researchers, delving into the collection of knowledge that suddenly lay at the tips of our fingers, long before the days of Google, Siri, and Alexa. As I communicated in a newsletter to the parents, "We are even looking up hard words like s-e-x." Now I could send my students into the encyclopedia to find maps and information about every country in the world.

One year, I posted three large maps in my third grade classroom, one of Florida, one of the United States, and one of the world. I asked my students to tell me where they had been born and each of us, me included, put a little red sticker on the location of his or her birth. We talked about what we noticed. Many of my students were born in Orlando, but many came from other states in the southeastern US and other parts of the country. We talked about how we could calculate distances on maps, why the three maps were similar in size but didn't represent their real size relationships, and that the United States is much larger than Florida and the world is much larger than the United States.

Next, I gave some homework to my eight- and nine-year-old students, instructing them to record where their parents and grandparents had been born and to bring it back to school. We put green stickers on the places where their parents were born, and blue stickers on the birthplaces of grandparents. It was fascinating to see how each one of our maps collected stickers, our classroom of twenty-four children blossoming into many, many stickers, distributed over a lot of area, in Florida, the United States, and the world. One particularly interesting feature we noticed was the fact that quite a few grandparents were born in Puerto Rico, but many of them had migrated to New York and New Jersey by the time the children's parents were born. Then, however, the parents ended up in Florida by the time their own children came into the world.

This observation afforded us a great opportunity to talk about immigration, why people do it and the hardships of learning new languages and customs. What reasons could there be for the Puerto Rico – New Jersey – Florida travel pattern? What causes people to stay put in a place or to seek another home? Why are The United States called a "melting pot," or sometimes a "salad bowl," and how are those terms different? And how do we welcome people from other countries – or make them feel unwelcome? Our very graphic map illustrations told us all a lot about our country and the people who have chosen to come here to live.

My third graders also studied Native Americans. As we discussed and read about the way the early Americans had been pushed off their land, I created a lesson to help my students understand the impact this had on the relations between the Europeans and the natives. One group of about half the class was designated as the Native Americans. I had them spread themselves around in an open area of the room. Then I began to have other children, playing the part of the European immigrants, walk as a group, coming in from the "eastern" side of the room and gradually moving further and further into the space occupied by the "Native Americans." The children who'd been designated as natives were eventually, and somewhat resentfully on their part, herded into a small area as their personal space was steadily infringed upon by the "Europeans." We had a valuable discussion of how our own Native Americans must have felt as that very thing happened to them.

A gift from a student that year is a potent symbol for me of the immigrants who found their way here and who have contributed to making America the country it is. Second grader Amelia was a hard-working little Latino girl whose mother was a young, single parent and a recent immigrant to the US. For Christmas, Amelia gave me a heart shaped pin with a little pearl in the center. The pin is made of gold colored plastic and the "pearl" is iridescent colored plastic. I have it still, a memento of a quiet, industrious child whose family found the money to give a gift to a teacher because education was important to them.

Amelia's gift

Transitions

• ◦ ● ◦ •

Education is learning what you didn't know you didn't know.

George Boas

Eventually, over the course of my years at Conway Elementary School, I taught several years in every grade from kindergarten through third. In 1991, while I was teaching second grade, my principal asked me to take training to become a math specialist for my school. This was a little ironic to me, as I had always felt my strongest teaching talents were in the area of language arts.

The principal gave me a wonderful opportunity, though. Through the math specialist program, which was an effort to develop nationwide math standards and improve math education in elementary schools, I had the benefit of mentoring from skilled math teachers, a generous allowance to purchase resource materials, exposure to nationally recognized math instructors, and attendance at regional and national math conferences over the next three years. In assuming the responsibility of math specialist, I was expected to make changes in my math instruction to model implementation of the national mathematics reform movement. I was also tasked with mentoring the teachers at Conway, encouraging them to try new math techniques, teaching sample lessons to their classes, and doing classroom observations for them with immediate feedback.

My assignment as a math specialist inspired me to return to college and work on a doctoral degree, still teaching full-time in the classroom. I began this phase of my college life at the University of Central Florida in Orlando in 1994. As I worked on my doctorate in Curriculum and Instruction, I took courses in Educational Theory, Statistics, Children's Literature, and Curriculum History. One of my favorite courses was Lifespan Human Development, which took me back to memories of my undergraduate degree in sociology almost twenty-five years earlier.

As time passed, though, I realized I was in danger of educating myself right out of the classroom teaching job I had always loved. At the end of this doctoral degree, what would I do? It was unlikely an elementary principal would be willing to hire "Dr. Thrailkill" to teach third grade or kindergarten, and I was not interested in becoming an administrator. With an eye to this reality, I took college and county in-service courses to become certified to teach gifted and talented students. For the school year 1997-98, I transferred from Conway Elementary to another Orange County school, Dommerich Elementary, where I would be teaching gifted students in grades 1-3 in a half-time position. After so many years at Conway, it was not an easy move but, by reducing my teaching hours, I could increase my college course load and inch closer to the doctoral degree, and by taking on a class of gifted students, I could get some important on-the-job training.

I was back to working with young children, albeit exceptionally smart ones. I began to learn how to channel students into projects that required advanced thinking and challenged children to analyze, evaluate, and synthesize, the top tier of Benjamin Bloom's Taxonomy. In 1956, Bloom developed a hierarchical framework to classify levels of learning. The lower levels are **knowledge**, or basic recalling of facts; **comprehension**, understanding the meaning of the facts; and **application**, using, or applying, the facts. At the higher levels, students

analyze, or break down information; **evaluate**, judge the value of information they have learned; and **synthesize**, create by combining parts of the lower levels to make new thoughts or ideas. My aim, as it should be in any gifted program, was to supplement, but not usurp, the curriculum in their regular classrooms, and to challenge bright children beyond the basics.

As part of our overarching study of the topic of "influences" that year, we investigated advertisements and their purposes. We examined and analyzed how written ads tried to entice us to buy products. One thing I found most interesting was most of my students didn't realize that famous people are paid for their endorsements of products. I think they were all a little disillusioned to learn that fact.

We did classroom research to find out which of three dish detergents did the best job of degreasing. We experimented with three different types of orange juice squeezers to determine (1) which one was easier to use, (2) which produced more orange juice, and (3) which orange juice tasted best. We graphed and discussed our results, and then the students planned and created their own magazine advertisements. By the end of the unit, I was hopeful my students were more aware of the power and purpose of advertisements in swaying opinions toward a product, and were more skilled at evaluating information they read and saw in the media.

At the end of the year, everyone participated in an independent study project on the topic of heroes and heroines as a way to conclude our investigation of influences. The first graders chose a parent or close relative and wrote facts about their subject into sentences.

Second and third graders had a heavier emphasis on the research and writing aspect of the study. After we had defined the qualities of a hero or heroine and created a sample list of real people with those qualities, each student chose a real person to study. They collected facts from various sources and planned a project to present to an audience of peers and parents about their chosen subject. We worked on drafts and editing and grabbing the reader's interest. After the projects finished, several parents told me their child's interest in the topic had persisted after our formal study. Yippee! Along the way, we took a side trip into a study of portraiture. We looked at some famous and some not-so-famous portraits of notable people. We especially enjoyed seeing a portrait of Mona Lisa made out of toast and one of Theodore Roosevelt created from soldiers standing in a field!

One day, one of my first graders asked if he could bring his violin to class and play for us. I happily gave permission and settled in to listen to what I assumed would probably be a skilled rendition of "Mary Had a Little Lamb." This pipsqueak of a kid played a complicated classical piece with skill and aplomb, leaving me with my jaw dropping.

For all of their exceptional intellects, though, these were still young children, and one of my favorite days with the first graders that year was April 1st, April Fools' Day. We had invited parents and grandparents to join us that day for a program. Snacks were served, featuring my favorite April Fools' joke. We had carefully cleared the frosting out of several Oreo cookies and replaced it with white toothpaste. The kids all got a big laugh from watching their guests try to figure out why the Oreos had such a strange minty flavor as we all shrieked, "April Fool!"

My year with the Dommerich students was an excellent introduction to the next step in my teaching career. My half-days with them taught me valuable lessons about understanding and recognizing gifted behavior, all while my college classes developed my own abilities to analyze, evaluate, and synthesize.

26

Becoming Dr. Thrailkill

· · ● · ·

Who dares to teach must never cease to learn.

John Cotton Dana

The part-time job at Dommerich Elementary helped give me time to finish my course work at the University of Central Florida. As it turned out, Dommerich was a serendipitous move for me, as it also gave me credentials I would need in my next job.

In October of 1997, my husband was hired for a job in Charlotte, North Carolina. We would be moving in the summer of 1998. Before we left, I offered my plan of study for my doctoral thesis to my doctoral committee. I wanted to investigate classroom teachers' perceptions of giftedness and the idea was approved. It meant I would have to be distributing questionnaires and collecting data long distance from North Carolina to Florida and back, but the plan to do so seemed like a feasible one, and my committee was supportive and encouraging.

My choice of this topic for study grew out of my realization that there was a patchwork of identification tools for gifted students being used in school systems all over the country. In Orange County, Florida, public school referrals for testing into the gifted program came almost exclusively from classroom teachers. Parents and students could refer but it rarely happened, and that route was certainly not well-publicized. There was no wholesale standardized screening on a grade level to identify students who would benefit from an advanced program. Once a referral was made by a teacher and an initial screening was done, the testing instrument was an IQ test. Students who scored a 127 or higher on the test qualified for the program.

Since the classroom teacher was the gatekeeper, so to speak, I was very curious about what caused a teacher to write the referral for a child. I knew from my years in the classroom that we teachers weren't formally trained to recognize giftedness. My own referrals were usually for the child who was a stand-out student, high achieving, and conscientious. So, what traits did teachers generally look for in making their referrals? Were those traits associated with student gender, race, or socioeconomic levels? Were there differences in a teacher's perception of gifted traits based upon the teacher's years of experience, or the grade level of the student? An additional independent variable was whether the school was a gifted center – that is, a school which served its own population of gifted students, as well as other identified children from nearby schools, who were bused into the gifted center once a week to participate in the program.

In the study I conducted, teachers responded to two questionnaires designed to define both their general and specific perceptions of giftedness. Early in the school year, I asked the teachers to choose from a list of twenty recognized giftedness traits four that best defined the term for them. This was considered their general perception of giftedness. In the spring, after the same teachers had referred their own specific students for testing for the gifted program, they selected from the original list the four most prominent gifted traits shown by each referred student. One hundred and fifty-six teachers provided data on a total of two hundred sixty students.

Among the most interesting, but maybe not unexpected, results of the study was the fact that student gender was a significant variable. From a sample size of 125 boys and 135 girls, boys were most often referred for advanced logic and problem-solving ability, talent for thinking "outside the box," and ability to think quickly. Girls were most often referred for advanced reading and writing ability, high expectations of self, and ability to think quickly.

School socioeconomic level was also a significant variable. Teachers judged evidence of advanced logic and problem-solving ability more important for the high or middle socioeconomic level student than for the low socioeconomic level student, whether they considered traits of giftedness in general or specific children.

Student race/ethnicity was another significant factor. Black and Latino students were referred in numbers well below their percentages in the school system (Black percentage of total population – 28.6, percentage of total group referred – 13.5; Latino percentage of total population - 17.7, percentage of total group referred – 10.0). They also passed the screening and the testing in such relatively small numbers that my data did not lend itself to further analysis.

The study fascinated me and had many implications for my practice as a teacher in the future. When it was complete, I sent the results to the schools who had participated and to the county administrative offices and the personnel of Orange County Schools' gifted program. I included a recommendation that the school system address possible issues of gender bias and racial or socioeconomic bias that might be influencing teachers' perceptions, and that the system consider a method other than an IQ score as the final identifying instrument for entry into the program. There was no response.

That was disheartening to me but I was no longer part of Orange County Schools and, beyond writing to the powers-that-be in the school system, I didn't see a way to impact change there. It was time to move on.

New Home, New School, New Job

Each life is made up of mistakes and learning, waiting and growing, practicing patience and persistence.

Billy Graham

During my course work on my doctorate, I read an article in the professional magazine, *Educational Leadership*, written by teachers of the gifted in Charlotte, North Carolina. Carol Reid and Brenda Romanoff described using Howard Gardner's theory of multiple intelligences to identify gifted children in the Charlotte-Mecklenburg school system. Their approach intrigued me and I communicated with Carol while I was doing my initial research.

With our move to Charlotte in 1998, I put in a job application to the Talent Development Department of the county school system, which Carol oversaw, and I was hired as a Talent Development Resource Teacher at Lincoln Heights Elementary, one of three elementary magnet schools in the county for students identified as gifted and talented. Lincoln Heights was an inner-city school, which pulled its student body from the nearby neighborhood and from students who applied to attend it from the northern suburbs of Mecklenburg County. Over the next twelve years I worked at Lincoln Heights, Thomasboro, and Davidson Elementary Schools, teaching children, mentoring teachers, developing and using curriculum, and testing students for entry into the gifted program, known in Charlotte-Mecklenburg Schools as Talent Development.

Right from the start, I was exposed to talented and knowledgeable colleagues. A few years before my arrival, the county had put some serious money into finding and training teachers to work with gifted students. Many of those teachers had been sent to a famous summer institute, Confratute at the University of Connecticut, and were immersed for a week - morning, noon, and night - in learning about teaching gifted children by top experts in the field. On my own initiative, I had attended Confratute in the summer of 1998, just before I was hired in Charlotte, so I was excited and eager for this new adventure in my life as a teacher.

I soon discovered there were very big differences between being a classroom teacher and a resource teacher. Resource teachers don't necessarily get assigned to a classroom, or even an office space. They may be assigned a space, but they had better be prepared to be displaced from it at a moment's notice, and reduced to carrying their teaching materials in a cart or a canvas bag. The space may be small, sometimes closet-sized, and they are likely to share it with another resource employee - a psychologist or speech teacher, for example. I soon realized it might be up to me to find a desk, a chair, a bookshelf to move into the area I was given. It really didn't bother me to hunt for my own furniture among the school cast offs – in an auditorium or gym or vacant classroom - and I was never shy about requesting the things I needed, even if they weren't offered right up front. That incentive to do what was needed to get myself settled in was the result, though, of many years of developing a comfort level with scrounging.

When I began at Lincoln Heights, I was given a small space that I would be sharing with the school psychologist. I moved a few of my books and materials into my "office," but most of them were left at home for lack of shelf space. My job was half-time, which worked well for me as I was writing my dissertation that year. Our office had a closet-sized room attached to it. The first year I was there, the attached room was full of art supplies the art teacher occasionally used. By my second year it was vacated, so I asked for, and got permission, to turn it into a small teaching space for four or five students. What riches! I could add another bookshelf and bring a bit more of the tons of personal school supplies I still had stored at home, accumulated over twenty-four years. Never be shy about asking for things you need!

A difficult aspect of my new position at Lincoln Heights was that I was a complete stranger to all the teachers with whom I would be working. Added to that was the fact my position was half-time, so I wasn't at school for all the same hours the teachers were each day. Both of these realities presented a distinct disadvantage in establishing a relationship with the colleagues with whom I was expected to work.

I decided early on that I needed to establish credibility with the Lincoln Heights teachers. To this end, during our workdays before the school year began, I made a point of wandering into the classroom of every teacher I would be working with that year and offering my help. If the teacher was sitting and cutting out laminated materials, I asked for a pair of scissors and sat down and started cutting too. I made sure to mention my own many years in the classroom as a kindergarten, first, second, and third grade teacher. I well-remembered, in my classroom teaching years, how I tended to think resource teachers did not know diddly-squat about working in the trenches of the classroom. It took a large measure of patience and persistence, on my part and the part of the teachers, for us to develop respect and a sense of partnership.

Gradually I found my place at the school and developed solid professional relationships, as well as some valuable friendships with my colleagues. The teachers in charge of the self-contained gifted classes in grades 3-5 slowly came to accept some of my ideas, to borrow some of the materials I had to offer, and some were even willing to team teach lessons with me.

In my second year at Lincoln Heights, I planned a lesson on "Ambitions" for a fifth grade class. Each year *Parade* magazine published an extensive article revealing annual salaries for a large variety of professions in America, everything from trash collectors to surgeons. Fueled by that article, we talked in class about what professions we thought we might enjoy doing. Following that discussion, I had everyone pick a name out of a hat. The names were those of adults I knew who were willing to write about their own professions. One was a business executive, another was my hairdresser, another a college professor, another my best friend who owned a Florida gift shop – twenty-five people from all walks of life.

The students and I developed a list of questions about these jobs, asking how an individual had ended up doing it, the training required, and advice they would be willing to give about the job. Each student wrote to the person whose name he or she had pulled from the hat, incorporating the questions into the letter. I mailed the letters and then we waited. Before long, answers began to come in. I was astonished and inspired to read the heartfelt words each person wrote.

My hairdresser, Christine Williams, wrote "I love my job very much. The good things about it are meeting new people every day, cutting and coloring hair, and never having to pay to get my own hair done. The bad things about it are standing up *all* day, and having to work *every* Saturday because that is our busiest day of the week. Whatever you decide to do in life, make sure you really like it a lot. Life is too short to hate your job."

Nicholas Kontaridis, a Greek man who immigrated to America in 1965, and became an adjunct professor at the University of Florida Center for Greek Studies, wrote "I enjoy teaching more than life itself. I like receiving the satisfaction of knowing I made an impact on someone's life, that I made a difference. I learned that it does not matter what age students you teach, you have to put in all of your efforts and, more importantly, love what you do. As far as financial matters are concerned, you do not become a millionaire teaching."

Every student in the class received a letter and the letters gave us all so much information, often about careers the children had never even considered. We had discussions about what education one would need to do jobs that looked interesting, and I felt the fifth graders began to reflect seriously about what the future could hold for them.

Over the years I worked as a resource teacher, I realized I missed the classroom teacher's day-to-day connection with students, the chance to watch kids grow and progress, and my chance to see directly the impact my teaching had on them. However, in my new position, I also came to appreciate the opportunity to know students beyond a single school year, to see them mature through third, fourth, and fifth grade, and to be a part of that process. I had begun to find my niche at Lincoln Heights, no longer the all-important classroom teacher, but still working in a stimulating and satisfying job.

28

Gifted Children – What do They Look Like?

· · ● · ·

The thinking of a genius does not proceed logically. It leaps with great ellipses. It pulls knowledge from God knows where.

Dorothy Thompson

I f I'm going to tell you about being a teacher of gifted people I will need to try to give you a definition of giftedness. However, this is an elusive concept and has been approached by school systems from many different angles, as I discovered during my doctoral coursework. Orange County Public Schools in Orlando defined giftedness with an IQ test, but tested only students who were first recommended for the program, as I discussed in the chapter about my doctoral research.

Some school systems do mass screening of all students on a particular grade level with a standardized test, and then further detailed testing of children with a certain score. They may use IQ tests, which measure ability, and/or achievement tests, which measure the things a child already knows. They may use checklists developed by researchers to help teachers with referrals.

I was attracted to Charlotte-Mecklenburg Schools because the school system had developed its own test to identify gifted behavior, looking at language skills, mathematics skills, and visual-spatial skills. A child could qualify for the program by demonstrating aptitude in any two of the three areas. All second graders were tested with this instrument, which seemed to me to be a vast improvement over the limited teacher referrals in the Orange County program. Charlotte-Mecklenburg was making an effort to find gifted minority children, who might be overlooked by teachers because of low expectations and the presence of racial bias. I was impressed with the county's effort, and eager to be a part of their more wide-ranging search for gifted learners.

As I showed in my dissertation research, even educators have different ideas about what constitutes gifted behavior and traits. Some of the most common identifiers for giftedness include:

Advanced reading aptitude
A love of learning
A good memory
An ability to learn quickly and easily
Heightened sensitivities
A talent for thinking "outside the box"
Advanced logic and problem-solving abilities
A strong sense of curiosity about many topics
An ability to put thoughts together quickly and express them
Creativity
Single-mindedness in attacking a problem
A high level of self-confidence
Flexibility of thinking

The best part of working with highly intelligent people were the daily surprises. I'm reminded of the precocious first grader who played a complicated piece on a violin for his classmates; the second grader who excelled at the visual perception game of Set; the many fifth graders who mastered the skill of thinking in a different number base with a little bit of help from me.

And, I will never forget the collection of four fourth graders and one third grader who had whizzed past their grade level work and who came to my classroom to tackle math beyond the usual. Together we investigated Fibonacci numbers, advanced matrix logic problems, challenging spatial puzzles, fractions with tangrams, critical thinking skills, deductive reasoning, complex Venn diagrams, Pascal's triangle – anything and everything I could find to present them with a challenge. I was rarely more than a step ahead of them, and sometimes found myself galloping to keep up.

The educational rights of gifted students

Just as we are obligated as educators to meet the needs of students who experience challenges with mastering academic material, we also have a responsibility to meet the needs of a child who needs more academic challenge in school. Programs for the gifted and talented are often in danger of being dismissed as an unnecessary "frill." It's a tragedy for that to happen, because failure to believe in and fund such programs runs the risk of stifling or wasting talent that can make significant contributions to society. Not to mention, it flies in the face of the goals of public education, the belief that every child deserves a good education. We must meet all students where they are, and commit ourselves to educating them from that point on.

A student who is gifted academically often has what I feel is a disadvantage in the sense that learning, remembering, and achieving come easy to her or him - often so easy that little effort is required to earn good grades in school. In an elementary gifted program, I felt I could contribute to the education of such children by presenting them with challenges before they got into the habit of just sliding along in school. Everyone needs to meet an obstacle at some point in life and learn how to overcome it. I saw my job as being an agent of helping children to learn to do that early in their school careers and, hopefully, helping them to carry a willingness to tackle difficult challenges with them into life after elementary school.

An interesting problem I liked to present to third, fourth, and fifth grade students was the card puzzle. Show the students you have ten cards, labeled 1-10. I used cards from several decks of cards, but you can make the card sets yourself from poster board or card stock, enough for every student or pair of students in the class. (Just be sure the numbers don't show through on the back.)

Show that you will flip the top card over to reveal a "1" and lay it face up on the table; then move the second card to the bottom of the deck. Then flip the third card to reveal a "2" and lay it beside the "1," and move the fourth card to the bottom of the deck. Continue in this fashion until the cards laying on the table are 1-10, in order. Tell the students you want them to arrange the card set you'll give them so they do the same thing you did, and they'll need to record the order they put the cards in so they can reproduce it for you. Sounds easy, right? The kids will think so, especially the gifted ones, and they'll be eager to whip it out. It's not easy, as they'll soon begin to discover. Eventually they'll begin to work it through and, as they do, they will demonstrate the trick to you to confirm that they can put the cards in the right order to make the trick work properly. (Oh, by the way, the answer to the card order is 1-6-2-10-3-7-4-9-5-8.) Most children will solve this problem by acting it out until they get the right order. But, I have seen kids who can reason out the arrangement by thinking through the influence of the cards which go to the bottom of the deck. For me, that particular kid shouts "gifted at logical reasoning!" For the child, or children, who figures the problem out first, suggest doing the arrangement again, but put two cards to the bottom each time. I'll leave it to you to figure out the answer to that one.

Grade skipping

Sometimes there's a push for an academically talented child to skip over a grade in elementary school. I've known instances where this is a good idea, but I'm aware of far more occasions when it doesn't meet the needs of the student. A bright child will still be physically less advanced than children who are a year older than he or she is, and this gap will persist as the child advances through grades. I feel it's much better to have that student identified for a gifted program, and work with specialists who can suggest and provide academic challenges to meet the student's needs, while keeping him or her with children of the same physical age and social maturity.

Being gifted and learning disabled

It may seem as though these two exceptionalities don't belong together, but they can appear in the same student. Frequently a teacher will miss a reading disability because a child with high intelligence will compensate with other strategies, and appear to be getting along okay. Because of my knowledge of my husband's story and my role as a classroom teacher, I was particularly tuned-in to students who showed exceptional skills in some academic areas but were struggling in others. One of my own children was a classic example. In his early school years, he worked hard but struggled to learn to read and spell. By second grade I requested testing to see if he had a learning disability although his classroom teacher assured me he was "doing okay."

At the after-test conference, the school psychologist said to me, "Well, I have good news and bad news."

I asked, "What's the bad news?"

She said, "He does have a learning disability."

I said, "That seems like the good news. Now we have an explanation for his problems and can work on them. So, what's your good news?"

She said, "He also has a high IQ and will qualify for the gifted program." Being identified as having two exceptionalities can present its own challenge. In many schools, students are pulled out to work with different specialists, meaning time lost in the classroom. In some schools, specialists are "pushed in," which means they work with students in their home classroom in a cooperative communication model with the regular teacher. Whatever exceptionality or exceptionalities a child qualifies for demands careful coordination and communication among the classroom teacher, the parent, and the specialists. A good resource for information on giftedness paired with other exceptionalities is a reader from *Gifted Child Today* titled *Teaching Gifted Students with Disabilities,* edited by Johnson and Kendrick.

Of course, not all gifted people display all of the traits that define giftedness. As hard as it may be to define giftedness in a succinct sentence, I've come to realize I know it when I see it, and I understand that many types of gifted behavior can be displayed in nonacademic as well as in academic aspects of life. I've also found gifted children are like any other child. They can be funny or serious, grumpy or cheerful, shy or assertive. They are often excellent jokesters, and I found myself appreciating the sly, dry humor so many very smart people have. I learned that, fortunately, you don't have to be gifted to teach gifted children, but you do have to be a teacher who is committed to doing the best you can for your students.

The Chess Club

· · • · ·

The beauty of chess is it can be whatever you want it to
be. It transcends language, age, race, religion, politics,
gender, and socioeconomic background.

Simon Williams

Early on in my job at Lincoln Heights, I was informed I would be
the sponsor of the school's Chess Club. *Me? Chess?* Years before I
had learned to play the game and joined my high school chess club but
that was just because there were a lot of boys in the club.

Nevertheless, I did know the basics of the game and figured I
could probably supervise fifteen or twenty chess enthusiasts. I sent a
note home with our kindergarten through fifth graders announcing
formation of the club. Permission slips poured in – and poured in
some more. At our first meeting before school, almost one hundred
children crowded into the school's gymnasium. All I can remember
about the first meeting was confusion – on my part and on the part
of the children.

Fortunately, I soon learned Charlotte-Mecklenburg Schools had
a partnership with the Charlotte-Mecklenburg Scholastic Chess
Association, an adult group of chess enthusiasts. The Chess Association
offered the services of one of their members to help teach the rules of
the game and get students playing together quickly. I found a corporate

sponsor who donated money for us to buy additional chess sets, and several parents volunteered to sew us drawstring bags to hold our sets. Our school's PTA provided the funds for our membership in the Chess Association League, giving us the chance to participate in local tournaments, and several parents offered their time to help keep things moving at each meeting. As we settled in, we met every two weeks and regularly averaged sixty to seventy players at each meeting, many of them kindergarten, first, and second graders, with as many girls as boys attending. I kept track of attendance and discovered one hundred children attended three or more meetings during the school year.

At the beginning, I presented the game as a fantasy with castles, knights, kings, and queens, and asked how many of the kids would like to be the commander of an army. There were lots of "Yes!" answers to that question. Right away, we taught the moves for each piece, giving students a page to help them learn them. We got kids playing as soon as possible, encouraging children who knew how to play to pair up with the novices. A pawns only game is a good place to start. It's a basic variation in which only the pawns are on the board, so students learn how they move and capture other pieces. Everyone can learn it quickly.

We had simple rules: 1. Be on time. 2. Be respectful of everyone at all times. 3. Be ready to play chess. We welcomed any student. We celebrated the club's accomplishments by publishing a newsletter, maintaining a bulletin board, and displaying the trophies our students won at tournaments. And, amazingly, we did win trophies.

In 2003, I presented a session at the convention of the North Carolina Association for the Gifted and Talented. I described our experience at Lincoln Heights in organizing and running a school Chess Club to promote diversity and walked the attendees through the steps we had taken. They took a handout home with them describing how we had set up our club with a bibliography to give them resources. Hopefully, a few more Chess Clubs were born as a result.

Participating in a county chess tournament

After I transferred to Davidson Elementary in 2002, I sponsored the Chess Club there also. On Chess Day, the floor of our media center was littered with boys and girls playing chess, and we adults had to step carefully as we wandered among them, answering questions and giving strategy advice. Here, again, parents were a great help to the club, most especially a mother named Karel Lucander. Karel was there for our meetings and also took care of our chess sets over the summer, sorting the pieces and washing them for the new school year. She once told me "for three years the beginning of school has been signaled by the Clorox dousing of chess pieces." What would we have done without her?

At Davidson, I had the idea of ending the school year with a "Tournament of the Giants." We would hold a chess game with human beings playing the parts of the pieces – Castles, Knights, Bishops, Queens, Kings, and Pawns. Students signed up to participate, and pulled from a hat to learn their parts. Parents could act the part of chess pieces too, and several of them showed up in appropriate costumes. I assigned four of our strongest players to be the Captains, two for the

White team and two for the Black team, calling the moves the humans would perform on a giant homemade chessboard out on our school's courtyard. After the game, we enjoyed punch and cookies (Pepperidge Farm Chessmen and black and white Oreo cookies, of course).

I came to realize chess really is a game that can have appeal for anyone. It teaches the importance of planning. It develops critical thinking, reasoning, problem-solving abilities, memory, concentration, and visualization skills. It improves confidence, good sportsmanship, and self-esteem. And best of all, in our school of diverse races, learners, and cultures at Lincoln Heights, chess transcended language and cultural and racial barriers.

Back to the Classroom

• • • • •

What we want is to see the child in pursuit of knowledge, and not knowledge in pursuit of the child.

George Bernard Shaw

In the spring of 2001, I took over the fourth grade classroom of a teacher who had left her job unexpectedly. My return to the classroom was exciting, but it was a lot of work and reminded me of the very first year of my teaching career when I came into a kindergarten classroom mid-school year, a little disoriented and confused. The students in this class, though, were among the most intriguing I had ever encountered – bright, inquisitive, and academically advanced, a self-contained group of gifted nine- and ten-year-olds. This encounter, then, was my first ever chance to teach a class-sized group of gifted students as their classroom teacher.

Lincoln Heights Elementary School was an old school and deteriorating in 2001. One day during a class discussion, several of the students complained about the rusty water in the bathrooms, the general heating and air conditioning problems throughout the school, and the disintegrating ceiling tiles in our classroom. They wanted to know what could be done about these conditions. Could we call the news, write the President; who could we expect to do something? I suggested we might contact the county commissioners of Mecklenburg County.

My students greeted this idea with enthusiasm, and I gave each one of them the name of a commissioner to whom to write a letter as a writing assignment. Their letters detailed our problems, suggested solutions, and asked the commissioners what plans they might be making to improve conditions at Lincoln Heights. I sent two or three student letters to each member of the county commission.

A week or so passed, and we got one response in the mail, a generic form letter from the chairman of the county commission. Then, a few days later, the school secretary informed me that Jim Richardson, one of the county commissioners, wanted to visit our classroom and talk to the students about the letters we'd sent. The next day, Commissioner Richardson walked into the classroom and introduced himself. He asked to meet the particular students whose letters he had received, and thanked them for their words. He talked to the entire class about their concerns for Lincoln Heights and the county's future plans for our school. He treated my students like people who really did have it in their power to make things better. With his visit, Commissioner Richardson helped my students believe social activism can pay off, and that ordinary voices can be heard by people in power. His simple visit did more than I ever could have done to teach my students that lesson, and I was enormously grateful for his sensitivity and his effort.

One day, my students in this class took an evaluation to help them determine their strongest of the eight intelligences described by psychologist Howard Gardner in 1983. Gardner's theory of multiple intelligences proposes it's more accurate to describe ability by analyzing the strengths people possess in eight different areas – verbal-linguistic, logical-mathematical, visual-spatial, bodily-kinesthetic, interpersonal, intrapersonal, musical-rhythmic, and naturalist. He felt that a narrow definition of intelligence, such as what we get from an IQ test, fails to capture all the many ways humans learn and acquire information. It was Gardner's work that had influenced the Mecklenburg County School System several years before to devise its own qualifying test for the gifted program, evaluating students' verbal-linguistic, logical-mathematical, and visual-spatial strengths as a way to identify children who would enter the Talent Development Program.

My students were intrigued to discover their strongest among Gardner's eight intelligences, becoming more self-aware about their abilities. They also came to realize that one person could be strong in multiple intelligences. I felt it was a benefit for my students to get an idea of how they had been identified as gifted, and, over the nine weeks I taught them, I tried to expand our areas of study beyond their basic curriculum, and into appreciation of other intelligences.

One of our projects that spring was the "adopt an egg" challenge. Students were asked to create a cradle to keep an egg safe for a week from Monday through Friday. The hardboiled eggs had to be protected from harm (i.e. cracks) and cared for throughout the school day. My intent was to help children get some "eggsperience" in how much work goes into caring for an infant. I'm not sure what the implications were for the future, but we had a lot of cracked eggs before the week was up.

As the school year wound down, I read aloud two of my all-time favorite chapter books, *Time for Andrew* and *The Prince of the Pond*. Although I had read both of them to my final third grade class, at Conway Elementary, I hadn't had nearly enough opportunity to share these books with other students. *Time for Andrew* by Mary Downing Hahn is a time travel tale in which a boy named Andrew inadvertently switches times with another boy who looks exactly like him. Andrew can't make it back to his own time unless he can win a marble game of Ringer, a game he has no notion how to play.

The story is a fine imagination stimulator, and also supplied us with a chance to debate the morality of choices made by the characters, choices that might change the future. At the end of the story, I gave each of my students a simple, homemade, drawstring bag containing enough marbles to play the game as a memento of this intriguing story.

The Prince of the Pond was written by Donna Jo Napoli and is a prequel to the old fairy tale, *The Frog Prince*. It begins in the instant after the hag has turned the prince into a frog, and follows his efforts to learn to live in a frog's body and speak with a frog's tongue, and get himself turned back into a prince. The dialogue is hilarious but, if you read this aloud, you must be prepared to speak as the frog does, mimicking his difficulty with R-sounds, a logical side effect of having a frog's long tongue. By choosing this book to read, I was encouraging my students to think "outside the box," honing one of those gifted traits that had proven so important to the classroom teachers I had surveyed for my doctoral research.

With the end of that spring I went back to my job as a resource teacher for gifted and talented students. When school started the next year and "my" fourth graders entered fifth grade, I told their teacher I felt she would never teach a more talented bunch of individuals. They had shown themselves to be curious, smart, engaged, conscientious, and always willing to rise to a challenge, in short, truly pursuers of knowledge.

31

Math Bees and Math Fairs

· · · · ·

The only way to learn mathematics is to do mathematics.

Paul Halmos

The Math Bee

After I had been teaching at Lincoln Heights for a few years, Kim Smith, a colleague in the Talent Development department who taught at Cornelius Elementary, told me about a competitive Math Bee contest she had organized with her students. It sounded like a good idea for Lincoln Heights too, and my principal was willing to let me try it. After all, my Chess Club students were now adding chess trophies to the trophy case in the front office.

Kim supplied me with math problems for fourth and fifth graders, and I sought the help of our third grade teachers to create problems for that grade level. Additionally, Kim put me in touch with a local branch of The Optimist Club. The Optimists are an international service club. Its mission is to provide hope and positive vision, and the group is dedicated to bringing out the best in youth, communities, and its members. This group agreed to sponsor our tournament and to supply us with trophies and ribbons. The Optimists also offered us the use of a light system that had been built by one of its members so students could push a button during our math contest to signal their readiness to answer a question. The light system was built in such a way that the first light to go on cancelled out those of any other teams. Sort of like Jeopardy on TV. Additionally, the Optimists sent a representative of their club on each day of the contests to observe the competition and to award the trophies.

During the spring quarter of the school year, teachers in all the third, fourth and fifth grade classes selected students that we arranged onto teams for the competition. As a magnet school, about one fourth of the students in the intermediate grades at Lincoln Heights were in self-contained classes for gifted students. Many of the remaining three-quarters of the student body were at-risk learners, attending the school from the nearby inner-city homes. We planned carefully so we had a mixture of gifted students and other students on each team.

On the days of the contests (different for each grade level), teams played elimination rounds until only that grade's winning team was left. These students were declared the math champions for that grade level, and each team member on the winning team received a trophy while all the students who had competed received a ribbon of recognition. The trophies and the ribbons were great, but we all liked to see the light system in action and the way it contributed to an exciting, competitive, contest atmosphere.

The first year of the contest, we broadcast it over the school's closed circuit TV. The second year, the contest was held in the school's auditorium and each grade level attended when its own group was competing. Of course, the contest was much more fun with a live audience. Several teachers helped the audience members benefit from the learning experience of the contest by having their students bring white boards on which to work the contest problems as they were presented.

The Math Bees were a rousing success. Teachers told me students who were on the teams were viewed by others as "scholars," part of a math team. The children chosen to participate responded by working hard to do well on the contest and by feeling good about their participation. For many, an enthusiasm for math was kindled by this contest. One of the best results coming out of this competition was to hear the next year's third, fourth and fifth graders begin asking when the Math Bee would be held as soon as the new school year began. They wanted to prepare for it and to have a chance to be part of the teams. Math had managed to achieve "coolness" at our school.

The Math Fair

The opportunity for students to be part of a school Math Fair is a good way for a child to get a chance to stretch his or her brain with a project on a math topic of personal interest. A few years after the Math Bee at Lincoln Heights I transferred to Davidson Elementary, and organized the Math Bee there, and also became the sponsor of the school Math Fair. When I took on the job of Math Fair sponsor at Davidson Elementary School, I offered to go into third through fifth grade classes to encourage participation. I asked each group, "What are you interested in? What are your favorite hobbies or sports? Now, find the math in that activity and turn it into your project." The result was a Math Fair of enormous variety, reflecting our ability to discover math everywhere in our worlds. A sample of a few of the projects students did – "Is a Puppy Really Free?" "What We Recycle," "How Much Time 5th and 2nd Graders Spend With Electronic Devices Over the Weekend."

We enlisted the help of Davidson College professors and former teachers and parents of former students to judge at our Math Fair. The projects were all displayed in the gymnasium and were viewed by the students and parents. The third, fourth, and fifth grade first place winners took their projects to the North Carolina Western Regional Math Fair in Boone, North Carolina, where they had a chance to look at the work of other children and describe their projects to more judges. The possibility of sparking a lifelong interest in a mathematical topic was very real, and the first year we held the Math Fair on March 2, 2004 we thanked our judges with the following poem:

On the birthday of Seuss, his 100th, we've heard,
It seems only proper to thank you in Seussicle words
So, for being our judge for our first ever Math Fair
Please accept our gratitude. We're happy you were here.
As you wrap up your judging, we hope you'll agree
That some words that describe our students are these:
With their math in their heads and their feet in their shoes
They can steer themselves any direction they choose
And will they succeed? Yes! They will, indeed!
(98 and ¾ percent guaranteed.)

32

Teamwork

. . . . .

Nobody among us is as smart as all of us together.

Unknown

Most of my Charlotte-Mecklenburg colleagues were already highly experienced teachers and they had a lot to offer me. They were more than generous with their ideas and, early on, one of them shared a fascinating team-building activity I used many times over the next twelve years.

The supplies I needed for this activity required between four and five bags of dried garbanzo beans (chickpeas) and one box of toothpicks for every group of five students. The night before the activity, I would soak the garbanzo beans in enough water to cover them completely. By morning they had gone from rock-hard to just soft enough that we could securely stick the end of a toothpick into a bean. (I've seen people use gum drops in place of garbanzo beans. I think the beans are a better choice, even though they require the prep beforehand.)

I divided the students into groups of four or five, and assigned each group to a separate table area. I covered the tables with newspapers, set a box of toothpicks and a container of the now softened beans in the center of each table, and explained to the kids that they would be doing a building activity. I showed them how the toothpicks could stick into the garbanzo beans. Their team's challenge would be to work together and use the beans and toothpicks to build the tallest possible free-standing structure. The last five words of that sentence are the most important to remember – they are aiming to build a structure taller than that of any other team in the class *and* the structure must stand by itself, with nothing aiding it other than the beans and the toothpicks. Each team would have five minutes to plan together how they wanted to build their structure and fifteen minutes for building. I suggested they make good use of their planning time because, once their fifteen minutes of building time began, *they would not be allowed to speak a word out loud until the time was up.* They could pantomime or write notes or diagrams, but they must not utter a word at all, neither out loud or in a whisper. Everyone on their team must be engaged in the activity to give them the greatest chance at success. Any team that broke the silent rule would have to sit without working for a one minute penalty. Not just the child who spoke aloud, but the entire team.

I answered a few questions before beginning and made sure everyone on each team could reach the toothpicks and beans in the center of their table. Then we began the five-minute planning period, and I made myself available to answer questions, but not to give any building advice. It's fascinating at this point to watch for the emergence of leaders as the kids begin thinking about how to put the beans and toothpicks together. Very often a strong personality will take over the planning, and tell others how she or he thinks it should be done. Generally, they'll realize they can make a Tinker Toy-like object, usually building on a square base, trying to make the base pretty solid and then working their way up to get height. I've noticed very little on-paper planning takes place at this point.

After five minutes of planning, I gave the signal to start building and the reminder that no talking was allowed. I've observed often eyes may slide over to other tables, but the kids don't really have time to copy someone else's ideas. They all work feverishly, building, sketching, motioning. I let them know when they have five minutes of their fifteen left and, then, at the one-minute mark, I tell them that time's almost up and to make sure their structure could stand alone.

It was always exciting when I called "Time" at the end of the building period, and went quickly around the room with a yardstick to measure the towers. Sometimes, the structures collapsed at this point, in which case I measured the collapsed structure at its tallest point. Remember: The structure had to stand by itself.

For the next part of the lesson, we all walked around the room and looked at every team's towers. We talked about what worked to make a structure sturdy and tall, and what didn't work. Then, I told the students to take apart what they had done, because we were going to do it all over again. This time, the planning period was much more fruitful and animated, with more advice and contributions from all the kids on a team. The building session went faster and was more efficient and effective. Almost always, a different group would build the highest tower the second time around, and our recap session at the end was more animated and interesting.

As it was first presented to me, this activity ended with the first building session. I added the second one because I reasoned it would give students an opportunity to learn from their own mistakes, and immediately put those lessons into practice. This harkens back to my own morning kindergarten/afternoon kindergarten sessions where I learned in the morning how to fix my lessons for my afternoon group, a valuable lesson for me. Also, with our observations of all the structures, my students now had the advantage of seeing the effectiveness of other peoples' building techniques. We were no longer leaders and followers, but true team members who had learned to work together. I observed that everyone had something to say, respect for everyone's opinion was greater, and the kids all worked to improve on their original performance.

It was a very satisfying lesson, for both me and my students. I think students benefitted greatly from the teacher's hands-off focus. It truly was a lesson of discovery with little to no teacher guidance, and it pushed students to exercise their imaginations and creativity, areas I felt it was my responsibility to encourage. It was, though, always a big cleanup job afterwards! The newspapers on the tables helped a lot as we could just roll the toothpicks and beans up in them and head for the garbage, but getting the beans and the toothpicks all off the floor were very important so we could stay in the good graces of our school custodians.

One twist on this lesson I never had the chance to try, but would have liked to employ, would have been to completely separate the groups so I could do it one time with all boys and another time with all girls. I was continuing to read more about gender differences in learning styles and was interested in finding ways to encourage my female students in science, technology, engineering, and math (STEM) fields. I think the garbanzo bean/toothpick project would have opened up some great opportunities to discuss the attractiveness of the field of engineering with girls.

Building with garbanzo beans and toothpicks

Supporting Gender Equity in Your Classroom

• ◦ • ◦ •

> Society as a whole benefits immeasurably from a climate in which all persons, regardless of race or gender, may have the opportunity to earn respect, responsibility, advancement and remuneration based on ability.

> Sandra Day O'Connor

I had always been sensitive about not assigning my students to traditional gender roles in my classrooms. What had once been very strict expectations in society about what was appropriate behavior for boys and girls, finally began to loosen up in the 1960s and 1970s. I was very much aware of the role I could play in carrying gender equality into my classroom.

As a kindergarten teacher who encouraged her students in play, I made sure to situate my block center right next to my housekeeping center. Cross pollination between the two happened naturally, helping both the boys and the girls feel they were welcome to nurture any interests they had in an accepting environment. One year, my kindergarten students were scheduled to attend a ballet performance on a school field trip. I prepped the kids in advance by discussing the art of ballet with them, by preparing them to see both men and women dancing, and by stressing the enormous physical strength and athleticism required of professional ballet dancers. Throughout the performance my students were interested and attentive. As we lined up and walked outside after the show, I was thrilled to notice a few of my boys were doing ballet leaps on the way to our bus. In addition, as my position as a math specialist evolved, I became more and more interested in encouraging girls to explore mathematics, feeling girls were not being sufficiently encouraged to see themselves as mathematicians.

Several valuable books added to my body of knowledge about gender equity, including *How to Encourage Girls in Math & Science* by Joan Skolnick, Carol Langbort, and Lucille Day, *Smart Girls* by Barbara A. Kerr, *Failing at Fairness* by Myra and David Sadker and *Mathematics and Gender* by Elizabeth Fennema and Gilah C. Leder. I read that girls' seemingly inborn talent of collaboration could serve to help them work on teams to solve difficult problems, and I put that idea to work when I formed a Math Club for girls at Davidson Elementary in 2003. Using a book titled *Math for Girls and Other Problem Solvers* by Downey, Slesnick and Stenmark, the girls in the Math Club worked together to explore the skills they would need to develop critical thinking.

I read that boys tend to score higher than girls on spatial tasks, and read an interesting article which addressed this difference. It proposed that girls have less opportunity to roam as children; therefore, less chance of developing a good sense of direction in the outdoors, and fewer opportunities to feel secure in moving and thinking about the physical space around them. That gave me food for thought, and made me feel, by being aware of such research, we can educate students to overcome some of the societal disadvantages that may cause them trouble in school and in life

In 2002, I presented a session at the North Carolina Association for the Gifted and Talented. Its title was "The Right Tools for Gifted

Girls." As I unpacked a real toolbox, I made the following suggestions for teachers and parents as I displayed the appropriate tool:

- Offer a screwdriver rather than a power tool - Resist over helping. Encourage girls to do their own thinking and develop their own answers. Teach them to recognize and use the control they have over solving their own problems.

- Measuring Tape - Keep your expectations high. Encourage girls to expect themselves to achieve, and to give themselves credit for high abilities and good performance.

- Tin snips - Encourage risk-taking. Once you commit to making a cut with tin snips, there's no turning back. Go for it. Help girls to embrace their own assertiveness and mental independence.

- Glue gun - Expect persistence and stick-to-it-iveness. Don't accept an attitude that gives up easily. Teachers tend to have lower expectations for math performance from girls, and our expectations may be dooming them to exert less effort in solving challenging problems.

- Shovel - Teach the importance of digging for details. Teach girls how to do valid research projects, using a multitude of resources, and how to pull their information together into a thoughtful whole.

- Ladder - Look for ways to help girls find mentors. Expose your students to female role models in the fields of math and science. A good resource here is *Celebrating Women in Mathematics and Science* (National Council of Teachers of Mathematics). Look for women in your community who are working in these fields and invite them to speak to your students.

- Blueprint - Give detailed instructions on the correct approach to tasks, rather than providing solutions. Watch yourself in the classroom. Do you tend to over-help the girls, give them less informative responses, or call on them less often? I was guilty of all three of these behaviors until I became aware of it.

Although the presentation was directed toward parents and teachers of gifted girls, it could have applied to all girls as we try to help them to reach their full potential. The influence of years of relegating women to a lesser role in society can be hard to overcome, until we recognize what we've been doing and work actively to correct it.

There are a lot of excellent children's books that will help you foster gender equity in your classroom, and will give boys as well as girls the chance to grow and develop into the best they can be. A favorite book of mine is *William's Doll* by Charlotte Zolotow. This book was published in 1972, and I think it was one of the first I ever saw that addressed nontraditional gender stereotypes. The William in the story is a little boy who wants a doll. His father is uncomfortable with this and tries to interest William in activities he sees as more appropriate. Even though William enjoys the activities his dad offers, he still wants a doll. His grandmother finally gives him one and explains to her son, William's father; that this will help William to practice being a parent and to grow into a good father – just like his own dad.

The Paper Bag Princess by Robert Munsch is another favorite of mine which addresses gender stereotypes. In this case it's the issue of the powerless princess who waits for a handsome prince to rescue her. The princess in Munsch's story is anything but powerless and, in the end, she rescues the prince. At this point, the prince gives her grief about her messy hair and dirty paper bag clothing. The princess tells him he may look like a prince but he's a bum. No happily ever after marriage, just the spunky princess dancing off into the sunset.

In 1995, I came across a chapter book called *Running Out of Time* by Margaret Haddix. Her very believable and very human heroine is faced with a frightening challenge, to save the children of her community from diphtheria. It's a time travel book with a twist and it provides upper elementary readers with a chance to tackle some difficult moral dilemmas.

As the years have passed since *William's Doll*, *The Paper Bag Princess*, and *Running Out of Time* were published, many other children's books have helped teachers to address gender equity in the classroom. *Once Upon a Heroine – 450 Books for Girls to Love* by Alison Cooper-Mullin and Jennifer Marmaduke Coye will give you synopses of 450 books featuring girls and women - "Kindred spirits who took center stage and held it." The book covers stories for preschoolers through young adults.

And Marissa Meyer's series of The Lunar Chronicles reimagines the fairy tale characters, Cinderella, Snow White, Little Red Riding Hood and Rapunzel in a futuristic setting where humans, androids, and cyborgs coexist. The four pivotal novels about the fairy tale characters are part of a larger collection, all written for young adults but appealing to younger readers as well. The books are action packed and the heroines are strong, interesting characters.

Job Sharing

• • • • •

The most valuable resource that all teachers have is
each other.

Robert John Meehan

In 2002 I applied for a job as a resource teacher for gifted and
talented students at Davidson Elementary School in Davidson,
North Carolina. I hated to leave Lincoln Heights Elementary, where
there were colleagues I had come to like and respect and students
for whom I had developed great affection. My last year at Lincoln
Heights had been part-time and I had also been a Talent Development
Resource Teacher for Thomasboro Elementary, another school serving
large numbers of minority students. Thomasboro was headed by a
talented principal who had been lured out of retirement, and she was
a remarkable leader. I was sad to leave that school just as I felt I was
establishing myself in working with students and teachers.

However, the decision to transfer was the right one as my commute
had become longer and longer every year. Besides the improved drive to
and from school, the Davidson job was a four-day position. I would be
job sharing with another resource teacher, who had been at the school
for several years and also taught a four-day week. I worked Tuesday
through Friday, and Amy worked Monday through Thursday, so we
overlapped three days each week. We shared a classroom/office, and

collaborated to bring challenging curriculum to students identified for the Charlotte-Mecklenburg Schools TD (Talent Development) program, and for other students whom classroom teachers had identified as ripe for challenge and stimulation. Amy Diamond and I were alike in all the most important ways, and also different in some significant ways. One of our most significant differences is Amy is tall and I am short. As we quickly worked out, Amy claimed the high shelves in our classroom and I claimed the low ones.

One of the first traits I noticed that Amy had but that I did not share was a neat desktop. My desk had always been in a state of organized chaos. I could put my hands on anything on the desk, but no one else could. At Davidson, Amy's desk and my desk faced each other, and it was impossible for me not to notice the contrast between the two. Gradually I was motivated to work to make my desk look more like hers. It was a change that stuck with me the rest of my teaching life. I don't know if Amy ever realized the role she had in reforming me.

The first room we shared was a portable classroom (a trailer), just outside one hallway of the main school building. On our first day of post planning, which is the day after school gets out for students, our principal informed us she'd just had word that our classroom was scheduled to be moved to another school - the next day - so we would need to pack up all of our supplies - immediately. The custodians would take our boxes to the auditorium stage for storage since the principal didn't yet know where we would be headquartered in the new school year. I'm sure many of you can imagine the panic this sent us into. As long ago as it was, I still remember being almost completely paralyzed by an inability to take action in the face of such a catastrophe.

Amy and I rushed to fill boxes. Thank goodness the principal supplied us with those and, long into the late afternoon, we kept packing. In the course of packing up our supplies and books, Amy came across a set of stuffed legs with striped stockings and shoes, looking like the legs of the Wicked Witch of the East in *The Wizard of Oz*. I don't know where they had come from but she had the bright idea to arrange the legs so they stuck out of the base of the outside of our classroom, looking exactly as they had when Dorothy's house landed on the witch in the story. We thought it amusing the movers who would be coming the next day would be confronted with a portable classroom that appeared to have landed upon the Wicked Witch of the East. Even in the horrible confusion of that day, we found time for a laugh together and left the room smashing the witch.

Job-sharing is one of those innovative ideas with which very few principals can get on board. Back in the 1980s, I had proposed a job-sharing idea for the kindergarten position I was in, suggesting another teacher and I could each work halftime with one of us at school the first 2 ½ days of the week and the other working the last 2 ½ days. I even suggested we might both overlap one or two hours midweek for planning purposes. My principal would have nothing to do with it, maintaining it would "be too confusing for the students."

At Davidson, Amy excelled at teaching Language Arts, and by now I was comfortable being the Math Person. Our skills complemented each other and our close communication with one another, with parents, and with our students, helped to make our position very effective.

We collaborated with classroom teachers to team teach lessons. We taught whole group lessons to classes, and we brought groups of children to our classroom/office for small group lessons. We made resources available to teachers, sharing our own large stash of materials and books as well as those purchased by our department. We mentored teachers and taught demonstration lessons. Together we handled the testing and paperwork for our position.

Opportunities for in-depth meetings with our teachers were hard to come by, though. We could sit in on grade-level meetings, but these were rushed affairs, often dealing with housekeeping chores that had nothing to do with us. I found often the best way to "meet" with a teacher was to walk and talk with her in the hallway, as she went to pick up her students from Art, Music, or Physical Education classes. Such meetings became all the more necessary once Amy and I were assigned to morning and afternoon car pool lines and hall monitor duty.

As an example of an effective collaboration with classroom teachers, in 2008, two of our fourth grade teachers and I presented a session at a North Carolina Association for the Gifted and Talented conference. Our presentation was titled "Not Too Hot to Handle: Teaming With Classroom Teachers to Explore Controversial Literature" and covered our year-long collaboration conducting novel studies of three books, *The Watsons Go to Birmingham-1963*, *A Long Way From Chicago*, and *Out of the Dust*.

The story of *The Watsons Go to Birmingham-1963* by Christopher Paul Curtis tells of a Black family that makes a trip from Flint, Michigan, to see a grandmother in Birmingham, Alabama, in 1963. The book is seasoned with lots of humor, but it also explores some of the serious racial tensions of the times.

A Long Way from Chicago by Richard Peck takes place between 1929 and 1942, and tells of the summer vacation trips two Chicago kids make to their grandmother's house in the country, somewhere between Chicago and St. Louis. Joey and Mary Alice's grandmother is the town's eccentric. She drags her grandchildren along on multiple escapades, but we also get a good picture of American life during The Great Depression and of family loyalty and affection.

The entire story of *Out of the Dust* by Karen Hesse is written in free verse poetry, an initial challenge for our students. The book begins with a terrible tragedy, and we always sent a letter home to parents explaining that before we started reading this story. Set in Oklahoma during the dust bowl years of the 1930s, the book helped our students relate to difficult family times, and a unique but effective style of telling a story.

After four years of our successful partnership, Amy accepted a job at a new middle school. I worried no one could replace her. But our principal hired Kristin Retort, and no teacher could have come closer to being a clone for Amy than she. She was smart, creative, and full of great ideas. For the next four years, Kristin and I enjoyed a comfortable partnership, planning, and communicating together with the same effectiveness Amy and I had shared. I was so fortunate to have the inspiration of both Kristin and Amy, two remarkable teachers who were consummate professionals and who both became valued friends.

I think the key to our teaming successes in this job was our constant communication with each other. We made sure to eat lunch together on our common days, to bring up any concerns we had about students, and to bounce curriculum ideas off of one another. We each valued what the other teacher had to bring to the table, and we were willing to use the good ideas we shared. Both of us were grateful to our principal for her willingness to support our job sharing position. Elementary school principals are so important in their role of finding ways to make their schools run smoothly. The job sharing experience Amy and Kristin and I had was an excellent example of a principal using flexibility to manage a job so she could keep talented teachers who together were more than the sum of their parts.

No Problem!

· ○ ● ○ ●

"Problem – A source of perplexity or vexation."

The Merriam-Webster Concise Office Dictionary

For far too many people, the definition of the word "problem" defines their attitude toward the study of mathematics. They cringe at the word "math." They insist they were never good at math and were never happier than the day they took their last math class. As I became more deeply involved in teaching and, coming to love the teaching of, math, I decided a much better definition of the word "problem" is another one offered by Merriam-Webster. That is, "a question raised for consideration or solution." This makes math a subject, not to inspire perplexity or vexation, but to inspire deep thinking towards the aim of finding solutions. Once I reached the point of approaching math from that direction, I adjusted my teaching goal to stimulating my students to learn to think, to deduce from evidence, to develop a strategy to reach an answer. I began to realize that in doing this I might not only help them to learn a better attitude toward mathematical problems, but I might also give them the tools to solve problems in other aspects of their lives.

There are many resources for teaching people to solve problems but, for me, one of the most useful was developed in a collection of ten problem solving strategies accompanied by problems, part of a series of books by Creative Publications, McGraw-Hill, titled *The Problem Solver*. The ten strategies are:

1. Guess and Check
2. Find a Pattern
3. Act out or use Objects

    ....

4. Draw a Picture or Diagram
5. Make an Organized List
6. Make a Table or Chart

    ....

7. Use Logical Reasoning
8. Brainstorm
9. Make it Simpler
10. Work Backwards

I've listed and divided the strategies above in what I came to think of as a logical progression of complexity, from least abstract to most abstract. Each strategy had a simple icon as a cue for students, and each requires very little explanation regarding how to employ it.

The problem solving unit was organized by grade level, beginning with kindergarten and going, book-by-book, through sixth grade. At the present time, I only find grades 3-5 available when I search the Internet for *The Problem Solver*, though.

I found virtually any math word problem, (remember, a question raised for consideration or solution), could be solved using one or more of these strategies, and I came to use them through a wide variety of mathematical challenges. However, I was very uncomfortable with the terminology of "guess and check," which implies a wild proposal from a possible multitude of answers, and then a stab at finding out if it worked. In some book I came across the term "try, check, and revise" and, for my uses, I replaced the "guess and check" strategy with that terminology.

What I think is one good example of the use of the "try, check and revise" strategy is the lesson I described in Chapter 8, where students estimate a number of items in a container and put their estimate on a number line; then have a chance to change their answer when they get more information about how many are in the container. Try. Check. Revise. This will lead a student to a more informed answer and will give him or her confidence in the ability to develop that answer. The process we used when we made the garbanzo bean/toothpick structures is another example where students got a chance to think about what else might work and make a revision. I see that as true problem solving at its best.

During a guided lesson, when we knew the focus was on a particular problem solving strategy, I might ask, after we had tried it with the focus strategy, "Can we solve this with a diagram, or by brainstorming with a partner, using a different strategy than the one suggested we use?" As students gained a deeper understanding of each strategy, they also became more adept at choosing the most useful one(s) for their purposes.

An intriguing resource is *The Hands-on Equations Learning System* developed by Dr. Henry Borenson. This system is designed to teach algebraic theory to students in grades three through eight. It uses manipulatives to represent and solve equations through balancing the numbers and unknown quantities on each side of an equation. I felt it laid an excellent foundation for later work in algebra, while staying at a child's level of hands-on reasoning.

Another good avenue in teaching thinking skills are the problems in the *Math Olympiad* series by George Lenchner. With three volumes a teacher has an enormous supply and variety of challenging problems to reach elementary and middle school students. Mathematical

Olympiad (MOEMS) is a nonprofit organization that offers worldwide competition for teams of "Math Olympians." You don't have to be part of the contests to use the problems with your students, though.

Additionally, when we want to stimulate and encourage problem solving skills there are many logic activities and games available, either online or for purchase. You can find some good resources from an online company called Mindware. Many years ago, I acquired a logic game called Logix, which I liked better than any other. It's hard to find now and the price is high. Several other logical reasoning games such as Rush Hour Traffic Jam, Set, Dog Crimes Logic Game, and Cat Crimes will give kids excellent hands-on thinking and reasoning practice. A resource for matrix logic problems, called *Logic, Anyone?* by Post and Eads, is one of my favorites, too, with its wide variety of good problems for third through sixth grades.

And even Harry Potter has a logic problem that is just right for fifth graders. In chapter sixteen of *Harry Potter and the Sorcerer's Stone*, there is a lovely dilemma worked into the story. Be sure you have figured it out yourself before you turn your students loose on it as author J.K. Rowling doesn't tell you how to find the answer.

I am not recommending these resources only for gifted students. I think any child will benefit from practicing critical thinking and reasoning skills. Find the level that's easy; do some problems at that level, and then begin to push toward more complex problems. Done gradually, many children don't even realize they've begun to think more deeply. This approach sort of relates to the story maintaining that if you put a frog in water and only slowly turn up the heat, he won't even realize he's cooking. Okay, that's a little creepy but, hopefully, you understand what I mean!

36

Outer Space Math

• • • • •

"I demand a recount!" signed Pluto

Written on a T shirt at the Lowell Observatory,
Flagstaff, Arizona, where Pluto was first discovered

While I was teaching at Lincoln Heights, I came across an intriguing resource. It was an adventure simulation unit called *Math Quest* (published by Interact) and featured a trip through a mathematically themed "Math Land," represented by a large poster. The poster was decorated with clever cartoon characters and the unit had amusing descriptions of the challenges children would face as they moved along the poster's path. Children progressed in teams along the path by solving math problems, thereby accumulating points to earn "gold" at the end of the journey to help their team win.

I paired this unit with *The Problem Solver* (published by McGraw Hill) and, over time, pulled problems from other resources too. My students worked to solve math problems each week when we met, and often didn't really realize just how hard they were working because they looked forward to the "game" so much. I used the unit with fourth graders at Lincoln Heights and at Davidson Elementary when I transferred there in 2002.

As we approached the end of the school year in 2003, I asked my fourth graders if they thought they would like to continue an activity like Math Quest as fifth graders. Their answer was a resounding *yes*, but they quickly offered suggestions for improving the Math Quest game. We had some discussions about new ideas and new themes and, before I knew quite what had happened, we were planning two new Math Quest-like games, one with a space theme and one with a mystery theme. I brought in two large poster-sized pieces of paper and laid them out on our tables. Over two class meetings I asked my students to choose one of several activities. They could draw characters and illustrations (in pencil) on the posters that would be the game boards; they could think up and write game rules; they could think up and draw outer space characters to represent the residents of each planet they would visit over the course of the outer space game. They got to work. By the time the school year ended, I had two illustrated posters, many suggestions for game rules, and a good sense of how we wanted the games to look and be played.

I collected a list of math words for fifth graders from the math text teacher's guide and from enrichment math material I had used in previous years. My lesson focus was always on extending my students' knowledge of problem-solving strategies and critical thinking skills, so I used problems from Math Olympiad, *The Problem Solver, Grade Five and Six,* and problems I hadn't already used from Math Quest. It was quickly obvious one game would be quite enough for me to flesh out over the summer, so I decided to plan the space game and use it for the 2003-04 fifth graders. The mystery game was put on hold, but I developed it a few years later and used it with fourth graders.

I named the game the "Plutonian Space Odyssey," and its story line was that residents of the planet Pluto were being challenged by the International Space Federation to prove they were a part of our solar system. Ironically, in the real world at that time Pluto was still considered one of our planets. It was not demoted from planetary status until 2006. I was a little ahead of the times in 2003 and had no idea science facts would soon be catching up to my science fiction story!

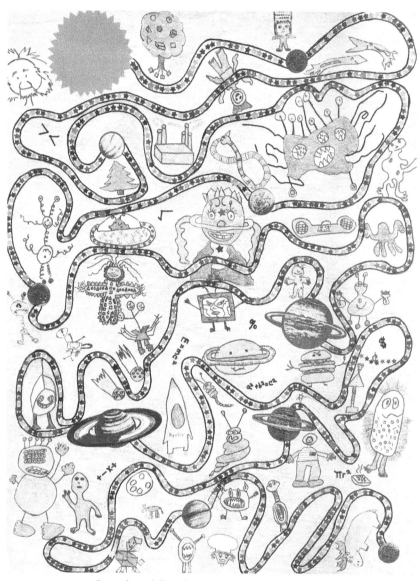

Game board for The Plutonian Space Odyssey

Over the course of the summer, I attached names to the characters the students had drawn. I wanted them to be funny and mathematically relevant, so I thought a lot along the lines of bad puns (the Black Whole, Polygon Al, The Prime Minister, Fat Chance and his brother Slim Probability, etc.). I colored the poster and created a path of around a thousand star stickers that wound from Pluto to the sun, passing through the rest of our planets in order along the way, and traveling around the characters my students had drawn and characters I drew to fill in spaces on the poster. I wrote a background story to explain the game and how it was played, planned jobs for each person on the teams, and developed the rules, based upon student suggestions and my own ideas and some of the rules we had liked in Math Quest.

So the mathematical equivalent of a hypotenuse must be a hippotemoose.

The game began with the pretend "purchase" of mathematically themed supplies such as a Googol Blaster, a Law of Averages, and a Negative Numbers Suction Hose. Each team member had 500 energy credits to spend, which was our pretend intergalactic currency, and all the members had to agree on what to buy. The supplies came in handy as, when all students on a team turned in their homework, the team was able to choose a fate card. Most of the fate cards were good while some were bad, often requiring the team to give up a supply item and/or solve a math problem. An example of a fate card is the following: "The Prime Minister will allow you to greet Queen Computation, the Ruler of the Solar System, if your team members can name at least ten prime numbers in thirty seconds." The characters the students had created the year before, with the names I had added over the summer, were incorporated into the fate cards.

Teams progressed along the path by earning points which were awarded by solving weekly math homework problems. As they passed each planet, they collected a picture of a resident of that planet to "help" them on their quest, some of which were illustrations the students did the year before and some created by me. The planetary resident pictures were glued onto the front of the team folders for a quick reference on how far the team had progressed on the trip to the sun. The object of the game was to reach the sun and capture a piece of it to prove Pluto had originated from this solar system. In our once-a-week meetings, I felt the unit taught my students how to approach math problems, how to select an appropriate strategy and also how to demonstrate their understanding of the process and the solution.

I played Plutonian Space Odyssey for seven years with my students. At the end of each year, we brainstormed suggestions to improve the game for the next year. In 2004 and 2007, separate groups of my students and I presented a session called "Building a Problem-Solving Game: This is a Job for Kids!" at the North Carolina Association for Gifted and Talented Conference (2004) and at the National Conference for Gifted and Talented (2007).

Earth's resident who joins the team, the Average Earthling

I loved it that my students enjoyed this unit and among their end of the year comments were the following:

"It helps you think more "into" the problem."

"Each Wednesday I would wake up and say, I can't wait for PSO today."

"You get a lot of problem solving in and you have fun while working."

"You stretch your brain in the homework."

"Our math program encouraged us to do better not in math but at the game but now we realize that our game *was* the math."

Their comments validated for me that, in addition to having a lot of fun developing and playing the game, students recognized they had been doing real math and it had real value for them.

Thinking in a Different
Number Base

• • • • •

Take me to your leader.

Alex Graham, cartoonist

After a few years of playing Plutonian Space Odyssey and teaching problem-solving and critical-thinking skills, it occurred to me our fifth graders might be adept enough in math to be introduced to the concept of thinking in different number bases. I knew understanding place value is an important tool in helping children develop a sound number sense - a comfort level with working with numbers that is the foundation for successfully manipulating numbers in basic math, multiplication, division, and algebra. If I could teach my students to think in other number bases, I felt it would give them greater understanding and power over much of the math they would encounter in the future.

We first reviewed place value and the concept that a numeral's location holds meaning. There is a one's place, a ten's place, a hundred's place, and so on forever and ever. Fifth graders find it's pretty fascinating to realize that quantity will never end; you can always add one more. That notion fascinates me, too, and I have no trouble conveying my enthusiasm for it.

We established that we humans use a number system called "base ten," meaning that as you move each place to the left on a whole number, you are multiplying by ten. We noted that humans come equipped with ten fingers and this probably explains our use of base ten. We studied a few ancient number systems such as Egyptian hieroglyphics, Roman numerals, and Babylonian cuneiform. We observed they became very cumbersome to handle as their users tried to write large numbers, due to the fact they did not employ place value.

We also observed the importance of the numeral zero, a concept that was not well understood by the developers of early number systems. The notion of counting nothing and giving it a symbol was a giant leap for humankind, and an important aid in developing place value because the zero can become a place holder.

Once we were all comfortable with this thinking, I proposed a situation: "What if you were to meet an alien from outer space and you wanted to trade with him? He offers you a trade: 2222 solar energy credits in exchange for your entire supply of Mardi Gras necklaces (numbering 350 in all)."

"Wow, what a deal," you say and you agree to the trade.

Then you give him the necklaces. But wait!!!!! The alien only gives you 80 energy credits in return! What could be wrong? Then you notice – he only has a total of three digits on his hands.

Could it be possible he thinks in a base three system? Considering that possibility, we think of our own base ten place value chart:

{10,000's place} {1,000's place} {100's place} {10's place} {1's place}

Then we make a base three place value chart:

{81's place} {27's place} {9's place} {3's place} {1's place}

The alien who wants to make a deal with us

Our number system multiplies by ten with each place to the left, but his multiplies by three with each place to the left. The alien has offered you 2222 energy credits in his number language, not yours. You can use his place value chart to determine the *value* of the number he has offered you.

In his one's place there is a 2. In value that is 2 x 1 = 2

In his three's place there is a 2. In value that is 2 x 3 = 6

In his nine's place there is a 2. In value that is 2 x 9 = 18

In his twenty-seven's place there is a 2. In value that is 2 x 27 = 54

$2 + 6 + 18 + 54 = 80$ so the *value* of 2222 in base three
is 80 objects, exactly what he paid us

Once we all felt comfortable with this new way of thinking, we realized it was a little bit like learning a foreign language. We practiced making other base three numbers, and then learned how to add and subtract in base three. I pointed out computers work in a binary, or base two, system and we work in a base sixty system when we use the minutes on a clock and in base twelve when we work with hours on a twelve hour face clock.

The unit culminated with a student number systems project. Students were required to choose a number base to investigate (not base ten or three). They gave their system a name and made up a symbol for each digit in their system. Their number system's symbols could not resemble ours but were to be originally created.

Students were to design a poster that included their original name for their system, the base they were working in, a key to show the symbols for each digit, two examples of at least a three digit number, written in their system, and each number's base ten equivalent. They were also asked to show a math problem using either addition, subtraction, multiplication, or division worked using their number system, and a place value chart of their base that included at least five places and showed the values for the numbers in each place.

It was challenging but fun to guide my students into this interesting new way (for them) of thinking. I'm convinced they carried this lesson with them into their math futures and it made them more powerful mathematicians.

Dear Dr. Thrailkill,
　　　　Thanks for a great year of MATH! I love PSO and working with other number systems like Hieroglyphics and Roman Numerals. I like the problem solving abilities that math uses and the way that PSO is done. It uses two of some of my favorite things: Math and humor. This has truly been a great year of math at its best! Thank you for a great year!
　　　　From,
　　　　Zachary Olguin

A typical fifth grade student reaction to our number systems project and to PSO, our shorthand for Plutonian Space Odyssey.

38

Mystery Math and The Rescue of Bad Luck Bones

• • • • •

"Elementary, my dear Watson."

Often attributed to Sherlock Holmes but never actually
said by him in the books by Arthur Conan Doyle

In 2000, I was inspired by another teacher in Charlotte-Mecklenburg Schools. Donna Yonkovig had created a mystery unit in which she had used several pieces of literature. I was especially attracted to student copies of three abridged Sherlock Holmes stories (*Mysteries of Sherlock Holmes* by Judith Conaway, Editor). Even though these are abridged versions of the originals, they are well-presented and are in an appropriate form for intermediate elementary students to understand, analyze, and study. Donna's work led me to build a unit studying the Holmes mysteries and a collection of twelve mystery centers that would complement and extend the story study for my fourth grade students in the gifted program.

Mystery Math

A study of mysteries is a natural draw for students of pretty much any age. This unit was meant to pull children in grades 3-5 into critical thinking and problem solving. It taught them strategies for deductive thinking, and gave them a chance to employ and refine multiple problem solving methods to which they had been previously exposed (See chapter 35). It was naturally appealing to kids; it integrated science, library research, geography and math; and it used many resources that were pulled together to make a comprehensive unit.

The working format for the weekly mystery centers encouraged collaborative thinking and independent pacing and learning. It held students individually accountable for their own progress, but monitored them closely enough that help could be offered if it was needed. I began the unit by explaining just six of the twelve centers. Each week I would add a few more centers, with explanation. Students were self-paced as they worked in the centers, which gave them control over their own progress. It also permitted children to spend extra time on activities of high interest to them, something we rarely allow children to do in school.

I did keep close track of student progress through the work products generated in the centers and, if someone was stalled in a hard activity, I offered help. I emphasized to my students that part of their assessment on the project was how well they could make use of their time when it was theirs to manage. I tried very hard to keep hands off as long as I could see there was progress.

The traffic in the centers was controlled with "tickets," color coded for each center. A student had to complete one center before moving on to another, and had to give up a ticket in order to receive another one. These were managed by student helpers because, remember, I wanted this all to be as independent as possible. The real key to success in this – and many other aspects of classroom management – is student training, making sure students know the routine and are comfortable in following it. Directions in each center were very clear so students never had to check with the teacher about what to do. (Well, almost never.)

I stationed myself at the fingerprint center because it required some teaching. By having one center that required my presence, I was able to stay in the middle of the action, but I was still placing responsibility for progress in student hands. When you make use of centers of any sort it's very important to have more center places available than you would need, so students have a real choice in deciding which center to visit. Having that freedom of choice is also important to me so I can see how children function as independent learners.

The twelve centers I created came from several excellent resources –

+ Decoding center – Before this center was added we did a short study of secret codes, learning about their uses in times past and practicing using and creating several kinds. My resource for this center was *Mensa Presents Secret Codes for Kids* by Robert Allen.

+ Mini Math Mystery – This center was one of the activities from the book *Math Mysteries* by Jack Silbert. I liked this book because it presents activities for students which require the use of the problem-solving strategies we were already using.

+ Visual Mysteries – A set of cards, *An Eyeful of Mysteries, 32 Illustrated Mysteries* by Mary Logue, formed the backbone of this center. Children chose and solved five visual mysteries from the card set, employing deductive reasoning.

+ Investigating the Media Center – The student activity sheet for this center reads – *Oops! A crime has been committed in the school Media Center. Five mystery books are hiding out. You must go to the Media Center and find five mystery books and write their titles and their authors in the spaces below. You do not have to bring them to justice; just find them.* After the students had all completed this center, I enlisted the help of a parent volunteer to type up a summer mystery reading list for everyone.

+ The Great Sherlock Holmes – The activity sheet for this center reads – *Of course, Sherlock Holmes was a figment of Sir Arthur Conan Doyle's imagination. Over the years, many people have tried to imagine just what he might have looked like. Draw a detailed picture of your perception of the great detective. Then make a list of seven character traits he had that made him such a good investigator.* Early results from this center convinced me we needed to spend some time distinguishing between physical traits and character traits. Teachable moment!

+ What's the Connection? – The activity sheet here was from the book *Powerthink, Grade 5: Cooperative Critical Thinking Activities* by Thoreson, Stohs, and Daly. It was a complex crossword puzzle that was a challenge for everyone.

+ Clue Search – I happened to have several copies of postcards of Norman Rockwell's April Fools' *Saturday Evening Post* cover in 1943. Every April Fools' Day, this artist made a cover with many errors, and students were asked to list as many as they could find (up to thirty) using a magnifying glass to discover the small details.

+ Fingerprint the "Crooks" – This center was from *Fingerprinting* by Ahouse and Barber and published by G.E.M.S. (Great Explorations in Math and Science). In it, I taught the students a simple, non-messy method to lift their own fingerprints, and classify them into the proper categories of arches, loops, and whorls.

+ Mr. Moe D. Lonn's Mystery – This center also came from the book *Math Mysteries* by Jack Silbert. The one I used here was a mystery involving the calculation of area and perimeter, a skill on which my students needed extra work.

+ Holmes' Home - In this center, students found a travel bag containing two large laminated maps of London, England, and assorted guidebooks for the city of London. The activity sheet asked students to answer five questions about London geography that could be answered using the materials.

- Calculator Tricks – This center had twelve activity cards from a set of 128 in *Calculator Activity Cards 3-6*. Students answered a question or riddle on each card by performing some mathematical calculations requiring use of the calculator. At the end of the series of operations, the calculator is turned over to reveal the answer to the riddle in words made by the upside-down numbers. This set of cards would not work on most of today's calculators, but you may be able to find a set that does.

- Baker Street Puzzle – This proved to be a very difficult puzzle for my fourth graders from *Baker Street Puzzles* by Tom Bullimore. I removed it from the rotation until some kids had finished all the centers, then offered it to those students as a fun, but very challenging problem they could group together to work on.

The Rescue of Bad Luck Bones

After I made the Plutonian Space Odyssey game, I created a fourth grade game for my gifted and talented students that was built around the disappearance of a Sherlock Holmes-type character named Bad Luck Bones. The story line was that the world famous detective, Bad Luck Bones, was in danger. He had been reported missing by his faithful sidekick, Dr. Whatson, and it was feared he had been kidnapped by his archenemy, the notorious Notoriety. Scotland Yard was baffled by the case and had turned to America for help. The fourth graders, in teams of four, were rushing to London by air to try to rescue Bad Luck before his luck completely ran out.

Now, if you are a fan of Sherlock Holmes stories you can see I was on a roll again, creating cockeyed cockney characters and bad puns to flesh out the story. The puns and the fourth graders did not click as easily as puns and fifth graders did (it's an age thing), but the game was still appealing to them and gave us a chance to do lots of challenging math which I sought to align with their classroom curriculum.

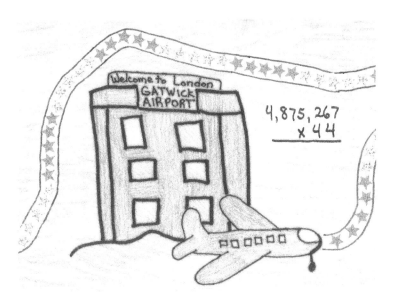

Gatwick Airport - The start of our London rescue mission

Our chart took the teams on a trip through London, looking in many famous landmarks for the famous detective. After "arriving" at Gatwick Airport we visited the Tower of London, The Globe Theater, Big Ben, Buckingham Palace, London Bridge, and Westminster Abbey, all the while tackling mathematical challenges with a mystery theme. We were helped on our way at each landmark by oddball characters such as Robert the Bobby, Officer Obtuse, Kind Mr. Mean, The Prime Minister, Invisible Divisible and Dog Cent, which had been drawn by students as we began planning the game in 2003. Each character we met up with specialized in a different problem-solving strategy.

For instance, the description of Kind Mr. Mean featured the Make a List strategy. The description of him reads, "Kind Mr. Mean, who will join your team at London's world famous clock, Big Ben, is just your average Londoner. His favorite food is bangers and mash and he enjoys a cricket game just like every other resident of this city. No one else is as good as he is at making an organized list. He spends most of his time organizing everything in his life, from sorting his socks by both texture and color and arranging the food in his cupboard in alphabetical order."

The players purchased supplies using imaginary British Pounds. Of course, all of the supplies had a mystery theme rather than the outer space theme of Plutonian Space Odyssey, such as a skeleton key, a Detective Society membership card, bouncing checks, a handful of digits, a magnifying glass, a cute little angle, etc.

The game proceeded as Plutonian Space Odyssey had, but with more of a focus on problem-solving strategies in the problems the teams tackled, and built around a list of fourth grade math vocabulary words. Here's an example of one of the fate cards from this game: "You will need a digital camera from among your supplies in order to earn 50 pounds and help Officer Obtuse solve this problem. If his photo album has 6 photos on each page, on which page is the 45th photo?"

We didn't have the chance to play the mystery-themed game for as long as we played the outer space-themed game. Within a few years, I was doing fewer whole-class math sessions with fourth graders and more collaborative novel studies, teaming with the fourth grade teachers. As a resource teacher, you want to be sensitive to the best way you can meet the needs of, not just the students who are in your program, but the classroom teachers of the children you serve too. By this time, the novel studies were the best way to serve those ends.

Primary Sources, Biographical Research, and Time Capsules

History never really says goodbye. History says, "See you later."

Eduardo Galeano

One of my favorite lessons over the course of my life as a teacher evolved while I worked at Davidson Elementary. This occurred during a study of nonfiction with a group of fourth graders. In addition to reading and analyzing many fact-based articles, the classroom teacher with whom I was team teaching and I discussed the importance of using original sources as we did research. Newspaper articles written at the time of an event, birth and death certificates, photographs and other documents generated at the time an event happened, are all more reliable in collecting and preserving facts for the use of posterity than anything produced later, or second-hand information.

As I thought about how to help our students fully understand this concept, I remembered I had a collection of documental trivia dating from my mother's life. As her only child, I had been the one to go through her belongings after her death. I had saved a box filled with odds and ends, I guess as a way of maintaining a connection to her. For the lesson I wanted to teach, I dug into the box, sorted through the odds and ends, and divided pieces of information into thirteen Ziploc bags. The bags contained my mother's birth certificate, newspaper announcements of her engagement, photos from her life, a few bills for things like electricity and car repairs, a handwritten note by her, her death certificate, driver's license, marriage license, and some academic diplomas.

I then proceeded to tell our students a little fib. I said I had come across a collection of photos and documents in a box in my attic. I wanted the students to examine what I'd found, and see what we could piece together to learn about this material. We talked about the obvious age of the documents and photos, and the need to handle them with care as we dug like archaeologists into these bits of a story from the past.

The students were paired with a partner; each pair was given one bag to investigate. For about twenty minutes, the kids gingerly removed papers and photos from their bags, took notes on the information they had, and interpreted photographs. One group was especially flummoxed by trying to decipher my mother's cursive handwriting. I encouraged the students who had photographs to not only look at the people in the photos, but to notice backgrounds (cars and homes), and to check the back of the photos for names and dates.

The next step was to go group-by-group and list our information together on the white board. The kids quickly realized that what they had centered on one person, sometimes listed as Rachel Nugent, and sometimes as Rachel Leonardy. The group with Rachel's engagement announcement was able to confirm she was one and the same. They knew where and when she was born and when she died, where she lived, the cost to repair her Volkswagen bug in 1967, and the amount of her electric bill. They knew her profession, where she worked, where she went to school, and the name of her husband. They knew what she looked like, and how she had changed over the years. By the end of the class, the facts on the board represented a biography of the person we had investigated, and everyone felt he or she knew her. The value of having so many small pieces of information that we could put together was obvious and every student in the room felt satisfaction at his or her part in developing the total story. Of course, as the lesson ended, I had to reveal our mystery person was my very own mother and to confess I'd known it all along.

Every time I presented this lesson, I experienced a wonderful secret satisfaction at reexamining my mother's life. It was a great research lesson for the students and a lovely trip back into memories of my mother for me.

Rachel Nugent – my mother

In 2007, one of the fourth grade Davidson Elementary school teachers and I decided to study time capsules. Pam Brunschwyler and I explained to our students that sometimes people like to bury historical items with a plan to dig them up later. The idea captured the interest of the kids. Each student wrote a letter to a person of the future, focusing on various assigned topics – politics, sports, entertainment, local history, current world events, and recent natural disasters. Most of the students added a small memento such as a photo, a map, a newspaper article or a small toy or sports trading card. On March 15, 2007, we gathered in the back of the school, near one of Pam's classroom windows. Students took turns digging a hole, and we buried the time capsule ceremoniously, recording its location on an index card Pam said she would save. The students decided they would unearth the time capsule in 2015, eight years away—the year they were due to graduate from high school.

Time passed. The fourth graders moved on to fifth grade and then we wished them a fond farewell as they scattered off to middle school. In the spring of 2011 they left middle school and by the spring of 2015 they were almost ready to graduate from high school.

Pam and I never forgot about the 2007 time capsule, although we both retired in the years before it was due to be unearthed. In April of 2015, the two of us got together at Davidson Elementary School, toting shovels. Pam's index card said the time capsule was buried beneath a classroom window. However, there were two windows, and we had no clue which one it was! We dug for quite a while with no success. We took a break for lunch. Some modern day fourth graders came to help us dig during their recess. Still no luck. Finally, I called my husband. He came to the school, turned over a few good-sized shovels full of dirt and, there it was!

The time capsule was stained orange with Carolina clay, but it was in pretty good shape in spite of its eight years underground. The plastic bag it had been wrapped in was worn but unbroken and tape was still wrapped tightly around the middle of the capsule. The words, "Time Capsule Do Not Open Until 2015," were still visible in faint writing.

On Davidson's Town Day in May, an annual springtime celebration, we revealed the items we found in the time capsule. Several of our former students were present as we took out all the letters and items we had buried eight years earlier. Water had seeped into the time capsule and many of the letters were damaged and hard to read. We carefully dried them out and returned as many as possible of the original letters to their owners.

With an eye to the notion that things might have changed by the time the future rolled around, the students had buried an interesting assortment of 2007 mementos - a golf ball, hand held pencil sharpeners, an eraser, a nickel, Elmer's Glue, a mechanical pencil, football trading cards for Charlotte Panther players, pictures of popular entertainers from 2007, a map of the town of Davidson, a Davidson Elementary PTA newsletter, Mardi Gras beads, and a Dry Erase marker.

The time capsule items also included a page from the Sunday, March 4, 2007, issue of *The Charlotte Observer*, covering a story on how several Presidential candidates for the 2008 election were trying to reach the country's young voters. Photos of Mitt Romney, Barack Obama, John Edwards, and John McCain were included in the article near a large advertisement of "today's coolest phones," ultra-sleek flip phones.

And there was a page from The Observer's sports section on March 4th, 2007, relating how Davidson College freshman, Stephan Curry, had scored twenty-nine points in Davidson's match against College of Charleston, helping his team head into the NCAA tournament. Ironically, just a few days after we found this article, Stephan was chosen as the NBA's Most Valuable Player for 2015.

Students wrote about many topics. One letter read, "Dear Future Guy, A big world event that happened in my life was the Indian Ocean tsunami." Another mentioned, "for the first time, an African American man is running for President (Barack Obama). Also, the first woman is running for President (Hilary Clinton)." The letters provided facts about the town of Davidson, mentioning one writer's favorite event, "Town Day...an event that parents and kids can have some fun." Others spoke of Davidson's Ben and Jerry's ice cream shop and The Soda Shop, two longtime town businesses that still stood when we dug up the time capsule. One writer talked about Hurricane Katrina, which devastated the Gulf Coast in 2005 and mentioned "to survive people had to climb on top of their houses." There were sports discussions and mentions of favorite actors, actresses and singers. The students' letters showed concern about global warming, immigration issues, and the war in Iraq.

Pam went on to do the time capsule project with two other groups of her fourth graders, in 2008 and 2009, both times with the plan to dig the capsule up eight years later. We again had trouble locating the capsule in 2016 but, with the help of the school's principal, finally dug it up. We never did find it in 2017. Fortunately, another fourth grade teacher had buried one for her class in 2009. She knew where hers was and unearthed it for us to display at Town Day that year.

By 2017, we realized we knew quite a bit about how *not* to bury a time capsule. Therefore, I wrote a page with suggestions on how to do it right, and we passed it out to attendees at that year's Town Day.

It was very satisfying to reconnect with our almost grown-up former fourth- graders. For those who hadn't attended Town Day, we searched for contact information and returned as many of their letters as we could with an explanation of what we had done. The chance to return historical documents and mementos to the students felt profound and momentous to both Pam and me. We felt our students benefitted from this connection to their past and, hopefully, even after so many years had passed, had a chance to reflect on the importance of our personal, town, and national history.

Davidson Town Day, 2015 and the Time Capsule is opened

How to Make a Time Capsule

Burying your own time capsule is an easy and fun way to create a link with your past. Here are some hints for how to do it.

Your Container

It's most important your container is completely watertight. We have found water can seep into just about anything. The best idea we've seen so far for a container is a heavy PVC pipe four-and-a-half inches in diameter and eighteen inches long with PVC end caps. Once you've filled the capsule, seal both ends with made-for-PVC glue (Oatey PVC cement). Sealing with duct tape or wrapping in plastic bags is *not* sufficient. On the outside, write in permanent marker the date you buried the capsule and any other information you wish to include. You will need to saw through the pipe when you retrieve it, making sure you do it at one end, and that you don't saw through any of the contents.

Your Contents

Write a personal message to the future. Include your full name and your address and phone number at the time you buried the capsule. Tell about yourself, your family, your friends, and your hopes and plans for the future. Include some timely newspaper articles about current events, and maps and tourist information about your area. Messages written in pencil survive better than ink. Photographs do not survive well over time in damp ground. Pack in some mementos – a snippet of hair from your dog or yourself, a small toy, a coin, etc. *Don't* put cellophane tape on anything. It quickly becomes gooey. Roll all papers loosely and seal them in zipper plastic bags (two layers thick is best) before putting them into the capsule. The mementos you bury should be in separate bags from any paper items.

Your Burial Site

Choose a site you can feel sure will remain undisturbed by future construction. Dig a hole about eight-to-ten inches deep, big enough for your time capsule to lie flat. Bury the hole and, *this is very important,* decide how you will remember where it is buried. You can use Google Maps to find out your latitude and longitude and write it down and keep that information in a safe place. You can place a big rock to mark the spot (this may not work well if there's a chance someone will move it). You can write a detailed description of the location and put it in a safe spot and remember where it is. You should have a plan for when you'll go back, and dig the capsule up. Leaving the capsule for eight years or more works well, and digging it up is lots of fun. Just don't forget where it is!

Spirits From the Past

· · • · ·

I touch the future. I teach.

Christa McAuliffe

As I write this in the year 2020, I am thinking back on my first class, the kindergartners I met in January of 1974. Those children are fifty-two years old now, with children, and maybe even grandchildren, of their own! I taught from chalkboards to whiteboards to Smartboards, and from mimeographed work pages to copier worksheets to computer assignments.

Occasionally a former student would turn up in my classroom at Conway Elementary in Orlando. When that happened, I would pull out my scrapbook containing class photos of my students from the past, and we would look this kid up in the album. We would marvel at how much this former kindergartner or first grader or second grader or third grader had changed in the years between.

How many children have I taught over the years? The number must reach into the thousands in nine different schools. You can never tell where your influence takes a child, and you seldom have an opportunity to see the results of your influence. To teach is a leap of faith that you can make a positive impact on children and their futures.

Sometimes a child's parents tell me if I've made a positive influence on their child's life, and that is probably the most satisfying "payment" I ever receive in this job. Once a mother wrote, "If I'd gone to the 'teacher store' and hand-picked my little Rosemary's kindergarten teacher, I couldn't have gotten a better deal." Those heartfelt words meant a great deal to me.

One time, a parent thanked me for letting her child know I liked him, while another thanked me for always being kind to her son. They were such small remarks, and yet they warmed my heart and affirmed the choice I made to become a teacher.

However, just in case I was ever in danger of getting too full of myself, I have only to remember an occasion a few years ago when I chanced to come across a student who had been my kindergartner in 1980. I introduced myself and proceeded to recall my memories of him. That went on for several minutes, and when I paused for breath he looked down at me and said, "I'm so sorry, but I don't remember you at all."

My middle son, Patrick, and his wife, Maria, went to the same high school. One recent summer they were musing about high school teachers who had positively influenced them. They both had fond memories of the same English teacher, James Lawson, and Patrick succeeded in finding contact information for him on the Internet. Together, Patrick and Maria sent Mr. Lawson an email telling him they both "regard him as their most influential teacher and can't thank him enough for his influence in their lives." Mr. Lawson wrote back to say the two of them were significant in his life also, and that he has nothing but fond memories of them and is elated they found each other. (Mr. Lawson also pointed out, however, that he had not "lost it" because he had noticed a spelling error in Patrick's and Maria's letter to him.) I was so pleased my children had written that letter to their teacher because I know, from my own experience, how much it meant for him to hear from them.

So may I suggest you take this opportunity to thank a teacher? Find a way to tell a teacher of the impact she or he has had in forming you to be the person you are or in having a positive influence on your children. Getting that thanks is so satisfying to educators, and it's impossible to understate its importance in affirming the value of the job we teachers have chosen for a career.

The following is a poem a child gave me as a present at the end of the school year. The author is unknown.

A Successful Teacher Needs

The education of a college president

The executive ability of a financier

The humility of a deacon

The adaptability of a chameleon

The hope of an optimist

The courage of a hero

The wisdom of a serpent

The gentleness of a dove

The patience of Job

The grace of God and

The persistence of the devil.

AFTERWORD

If you've found a job you really like, you'll
never have to work a day in your life.

Unknown

Some final advice from wise, old, and experienced teachers:

1. Every child deserves a chance for a fresh start every school year.

   When you get your new class list, *don't* go and ask last year's teachers to tell you about your new students before you meet them.

2. Grade papers with a green pen. Green is so much more appealing than red.

3. Keep a healthy supply of good pencil erasers. You and your students will need them.

4. Read aloud to your students, no matter what their ages are.

5. Before you ask, "Why would we do this?" ask 'Why not do it?" Open yourself to new possibilities.

6. Students from all ability levels will benefit from instruction in developing thinking and reasoning skills.

7. Be fair.

8. Teach your students from where they are to where you want them to be.

9. Never hold a difficult parent against a child.

10. Treat other people the way you want them to treat you.

It was at the beginning of the 2009-2010 school year when I felt I might be ready to retire from teaching. All that year – the ever exciting first day of school, helping with the newspaper club, organizing the Math Fair, teaching my challenging and always interesting students - I kept thinking, "This could be the last time you do this, Colleen." By midyear, I was comfortable with that thought, and ready to get serious about leaving this career I've loved since I entered it in 1974. By June I was ready to go - and I went.

No more early morning risings. No more stacks of papers to grade, no more endless meetings, no more deadlines to meet. I now could enjoy leisurely lunches, no longer gulping my food down in twenty minutes. It was intoxicating to have so much free time and I reveled in not living to a schedule. I could even forego wearing a watch! This was a major life change after, literally, living on "school time" ever since I was a three-year-old and entered preschool.

My husband and I had purchased a forty-two-foot power boat just before we retired, and we began to spend our winters living on it and cruising throughout Florida. Even though Wayne and I were enjoying retirement together, I soon missed the company of children. One winter, while we were docked in Vero Beach, Florida, I found an opportunity to volunteer as a judge for the Indian River Regional Science and Engineering Fair, and I returned to do it again for the next couple of years.

After a few years of retirement, I contacted some of my former colleagues at Davidson Elementary about volunteering in their classrooms. Several of them took me up on my offer and, as I write this, my Tuesdays have been devoted to helping in classrooms, and creating and teaching novel studies for eight years.

Not long after I retired, the town of Davidson started offering a lifelong learning program called DavidsonLearns. I took several classes through the program – one on memoir writing titled, "It's My Story and I'm Stickin' to It," another one exploring genealogy, and a poetry class. I enjoyed the idea of these classes so much that I asked the director of the program, Amy Diamond, if she had considered offering a class in grandparenting.

She replied, "Do you want to teach it?'

My immediate reaction was, "Heck, no" but the word that came to mind was a little stronger than "heck." On closer examination I thought, "Why not?" I'm the devoted grandmother of four grandchildren and I have a good notion about how to do that job. I created a proposal and, to date have taught four sessions of "21st Century Grandparenting in the United States" for DavidsonLearns.

A treasured retirement memory I have is of the weekend a few years ago with my granddaughters, Jackie and Kate. We spent hours with the girls' American Girl dolls playing "school." Jackie was the teacher and Kate and I were her not-always-well-behaved students. What fun it was for me to act out that role reversal!

I guess there's no cure for it. I am, and always will be a lifelong teacher and student.

REFERENCES

Resources for Teachers

Abrohms, A. (1992). *Literature-based math activities: An integrated approach.* Scholastic, NY, NY.

Ahouse, J. & Barber, J. (2000). *Fingerprinting* from G.E.M.S. (Great Explorations in Math and Science. Lawrence Hall of Science, Berkeley, CA.

Allen, R. (1996). *Mensa presents secret codes for kids.* Barnes & Noble Books, NY, NY.

Baratta-Lorton, M. (1994). *Mathematics their way.* Pearson Education, NY, NY.

Baratta-Lorton, M. (unknown). *Workjobs: Activity-Centered Learning for Early Childhood Education.* No longer available from Pearson Education. Can be accessed through Amazon.com.

Bloom, B. (1956). *Taxonomy of educational objectives.* Addison-Wesley Publishing, Boston, MA.

Borenson, H. (1986). *Hands-on equations learning system.* Borenson and Associates, Allentown, PA.

Bullimore, T. (1992). *Baker Street puzzles.* Sterling Publishing, NY, NY.

Burk, D., Snider, A. & Symonds, P. (1991). *Math excursions 2.* Heinemann, Portsmouth, NH.

Burns, M. (1992). *About teaching mathematics*. Math Solutions Publications, Houghton Mifflin Harcourt, Boston, MA.

Burns, M. & Sheffield, S. (2004). *Math and literature: Grades K-3*. Math Solutions Publications, Houghton Mifflin Harcourt, Boston, MA.

Burns, M. (1982). *Math for smarty pants*. Scholastic, NY, NY.

Burns, M. (1975). *The I hate mathematics! book*. Scholastic, NY, NY.

Clyne, M. & Griffiths, R. (1991). *Books you can count on: Linking mathematics and literature*. Heinemann, Portsmouth, NH.

Cooney, M. P. (Ed.) (1996). *Celebrating women in mathematics and science*. National Council of Teachers of Mathematics, Reston, VA.

Cooper-Mullin, A. & Coye, J. (1998). *Once Upon a Heroine*. Contemporary Books, Chicago, IL.

Dahl, R. (1988). *Matilda*. Jonathan Cape, London.

Downie, D., Slesnick, T., & Stenmark, J. (1981). *Math for girls and other problem solvers*: EQUALS, Lawrence Hall of Science, Berkeley, CA.

Fennema, E. & Leder, G., (Eds.) (1990). *Mathematics and gender*. Teachers College Press, NY, NY.

Frost, R. (1967). *Robert Frost's poems*. Simon & Schuster, NY, NY.

Gardner, H. (1983). *Frames of mind: The theory of multiple intelligences*. Basic Books, NY, NY.

Griffin, J. (1961). *Black like me*. Houghton Mifflin Harcourt, Boston, MA.

Irvin, B. (1995). *Geometry and Fractions with Pattern Blocks, Grade 3-6*. Learning Resources, Vernon Hills, IL.

Irvin, B. (1995). *Geometry and Fractions with Tangrams, Grade 3-6.* Learning Resources, Vernon Hills, IL.

Johnsen, S. & Kendrick, J., (Eds.) (2005). *Teaching Gifted Students with Disabilities.* Prufrock Press, Waco, TX.

Kaplan-Lyss, C. & Becker, S. (1987). *Stone soup – A "rock" opera.* Lorenz Educational Press, Dayton, OH.

Kerr, B. (1994). *Smart girls.* Gifted Psychology Press, Scottsdale, AZ.

Kozol, J. (1991). *Savage Inequalities.* Crown Publishers, NY, NY.

Lenchner, G. (1997). *Math Olympiad contest problems for elementary and middle schools.* Glenwood Publications, East Meadow, NY.

Lenchner, G. (2008). *Math Olympiad contest problems, Vol II.* Glenwood Publications, East Meadow, NY.

Lenchner, G. (1983). *Creative problem solving in school mathematics, Second edition.* Glenwood Publications, East Meadow, NY.

Logue, M. (1995). *An eyeful of mysteries: 32 illustrated mysteries.* JM Voigt.

Math Quest. Interact, 1914 Palomar Oaks Way, Suite 150, Carlsbad, CA 92008. (Phone 1-800-359-0961, Item #5078C2)

Post, B. & Eads, S. (1982) *Logic, anyone?* Makemaster Books.

The Problem Solver, Grades 4, 5, & 6. McGraw Hill/Wright Group. Creative Publications, Chicago, IL 60601.

Reid, C. & Romanoff, B. (1997). Using multiple intelligence theory to identify gifted children. *Educational Leadership, 55,* (1), 71-74.

Sadker, M. & Sadker, D. (1994). *Failing at fairness.* Simon & Schuster, NY, NY.

Silbert, J. (1995). *Math mysteries: stories and activities to build problem-solving skills.* Scholastic, NY, NY.

Skolnick, J., Langbort, C. & Day, L. (1982). *How to encourage girls in math & science.* Dale Seymour Publications, Palo Alto, CA.

Thoreson, K., Stohs, A., Daly, L. & Barden, C. (2000). *Powerthink: cooperative critical thinking activities.* Frank Schaffer, Torrence, CA.

Thrailkill, C. (1999). An *exploration of elementary level classroom teachers' perceptions of giftedness.* Doctoral dissertation: University of Central Florida, Orlando, FL.

Trelease, J. (1979). *The read-aloud handbook.* Originally self-published, later editions by Penguin, Random House, NY, NY.

Books for Children

Banks, L.R. (1980). *The Indian in the Cupboard.* Avon Books, NY, NY.

Banks, S. (1993). *Remember my Name.* Scholastic, NY, NY.

Baum, L. F. (1900). *The Wizard of Oz.* George M. Hill, Chicago, IL.

Brown, M. (1947). *Stone Soup.* Simon & Schuster, NY, NY.

Brumbeau, J. (2000). *The Quiltmaker's Gift.* Pfeifer-Hamilton, Duluth, MN.

Caple, K. (1986). *The Purse.* Houghton Mifflin Harcourt, Boston, MA.

Cleary, B. (1984). The Ramona Quimby books. William Morrow Publishing, NY, NY.

Conaway, J. (ED.) (1982). *Mysteries of Sherlock Holmes.* Random House, NY, NY.

Curtis, C.P. (1995). *The Watsons go to Birmingham*. Random House, NY, NY.

Cuyler, M. (2000). *100th Day Worries*. Scholastic, NY, NY.

Dallas, S. (2008). *Tallgrass*. St. Martin's Press, NY, NY.

Good, M. (1999). *Reuben and the Quilt*. Good Books, Intercourse, PA.

Haddix, M. (1995). *Running out of Time*. Simon & Schuster, NY, NY.

Hahn, M.D. (1994). *Time for Andrew*. Avon Books, NY, NY.

Hesse, K. (1997). *Out of the Dust*. Scholastic, NY, NY.

Hutchins, P. (1986). *The Doorbell Rang*. Greenwillow Books, NY, NY.

Johnston, T. (1985). *The Quilt Story*. G.P. Putnam's, NY, NY.

Jonas, A. (1983). *Round Trip*. Scholastic, NY, NY.

Kelly, E. (1928). *The Trumpeter of Krakow*. Simon & Schuster, NY, NY.

Knight, H. (1981). *The Twelve Days of Christmas*. Macmillan Publishers, NY, NY.

Lobel, A. (1970). *Frog and Toad are Friends*. HarperCollins Publishers, NY, NY.

Matthews, L. (1979). *Gator Pie*. Dodd, Mead & Company, NY, NY.

McGovern, A. (1968). *Stone Soup*. Scholastic, NY, NY.

Mayer, M. (1974). *Frog Goes to Dinner*. Scholastic, NY, NY.

Meyer, M. (2012). *Cinder*. Macmillan Publishers, NY, NY.

Meyer, M. (2013). *Scarlet*. Macmillan Publishers, NY, NY.

Meyer, M. (2014). *Cress*. Macmillan Publishers, NY, NY.

Meyer, M. (2015). *Winter.* Macmillan Publishers, NY, NY.

Minarik, E. (1961). *Little Bear's Visit.* Harper & Row, NY, NY.

Munsch, R. (1988). *Angela's Airplane.* Annick Press, Toronto, Ontario, Canada.

Munsch, R. (1983). *David's Father.* Annick Press, Toronto, Ontario, Canada.

Munsch, R. (1990). *Something Good.* Annick Press, Toronto, Ontario, Canada.

Munsch, R. (1980). *The Paper Bag Princess.* Annick Press, Toronto, Ontario, Canada.

Munsch, R. & Askar, S. (1995). *From Far Away.* Annick Press, Toronto, Ontario, Canada.

Myller, R. (1962). *How Big is a Foot?* Penguin Random House, NY, NY.

Napoli, D. (1992). *The Prince of the Pond.* Puffin Books, NY, NY.

Paulsen, G. (1999). *Hatchet.* Simon & Schuster, NY, NY.

Peck, R. (1998). *A Long Way from Chicago.* Scholastic, NY, NY.

Polacco, P. (1988). *The Keeping Quilt.* The Trumpet Club, NY, NY.

Polacco, P. (1998). *Thank You, Mr. Falker.* Philomel Books, NY, NY.

Rawls, W. (1961). *Where the Red Fern Grows.* Doubleday, NY, NY.

Ross, T. (1987). *Stone Soup.* Penguin Books NY, NY.

Rowling, J. (1997). *Harry Potter and the Sorcerer's Stone.* Scholastic, NY, NY.

Sachar, L. (1998). *Holes.* Scholastic, NY, NY.

Sachar, L. (1978). *Sideways Stories from Wayside School*. Scholastic, NY, NY.

Seuss, Dr. (1963). *Dr. Seuss's ABC*. Random House, NY, NY.

Seuss, Dr. (1938). *The 500 Hats of Bartholomew Cubbins*. Random House, NY, NY.

Seuss, Dr. (1990). *Oh, the Places You'll Go*. Random House, NY, NY.

Silverstein, S. (1974). *Where the Sidewalk Ends*. HarperCollins Publishers, NY, NY.

Silverstein, S. (1981). A *Light in the Attic*. HarperCollins Publishers, NY, NY.

Slobodkina, E. (1947). *Caps for Sale*. HarperCollins Publishers, NY, NY.

Stuart, M. (1960). *The Pirates' Bridge*. Lothrop, Lee & Shepard, NY, NY.

Tompert, A. (1990). *Grandfather Tang's Story*. Crown Publishers, NY, NY.

Viorst, J. (1978) *Alexander, Who Used to Be Rich Last Sunday*. Scholastic, NY, NY.

Wilder, L.I. (1932). *Little House in the Big Woods*. HarperCollins Publishers, NY, NY.

White, E.B. (1952). *Charlotte's Web*. HarperCollins Publishers, NY, NY.

Wood, A. (1984). *The Napping House*. Harcourt, Brace, Jovanovish Publishers, Orlando, FL.

Zolotow, C. (1972). *William's Doll*. Harper & Row, NY, NY.

APPENDIX

Perfect Play Dough

(Chapter 3 - What do You do in Kindergarten? & Chapter 5 - Classroom Management)

    2 cups flour
    ½ cup salt
    1 Tbsp. cream of tartar
    1 ¾ cup warm water
    2 Tbsp. vegetable oil
    Food coloring

Directions: In a medium pot, combine flour, salt, and cream of tartar. Mix well with a spoon. Combine water and food coloring; then mix this and the oil into the dry ingredients. Bring to a boil over medium heat, stirring constantly. When it thickens to a play dough consistency, turn it out onto a table and knead until smooth. If you make this with a group of children, let it cool a little, then give each child a portion to knead and to play with.

Store in an airtight container or plastic bag.

Stone Soup

(Chapter 4 – Half-Day Kindergarten to Full-Day Kindergarten)

1 large, well, washed stone
About ½ lb. of stew meat, chopped up and browned ahead of time
1 Tbsp. olive oil
2-3 carrots, chopped
3-4 potatoes, peeled and chopped
1 small onion, chopped
Salt and pepper
4-5 cups of beef broth
Some water

Put the stone into a large kettle and then add the rest of ingredients as they are mentioned in the story. (Some versions don't include the beef, but it gives it a good flavor.) Bring to a simmer and cook for several hours, until the vegetables are tender. Serve to children in a tiny paper cup. They can usually be convinced to eat a tiny amount even if they don't think they'll like it, and most will come back for more.

Make your own fraction kit

(Chapter 8 – The Place for Math Manipulatives in the Classroom & Chapter 20 – Parent/Teacher Relations)

1. Cut 12" x 18" construction paper of five different colors into 3" x 18" strips, enough for one strip of each color for each child in your class.

2. The teacher chooses one color to be one whole, and has each child initial one of that color and set it aside. You can label it 1/1 which will help in your later teaching. Refer to it as "one whole."

3. Choose another color (the same for everyone) and have each child fold it in half and cut on the center line. These pieces are each ½ and are labeled as such. Again, children put their initials on each piece.

4. Choose another color and have students fold it into four equal pieces, first in half and then in half again. Label each of these ¼. Initial each piece again.

5. With another color, carefully fold a strip in half, cut, fold each in half again, cut, fold each in half again and cut and we have eighths. Label each 1/8 and initial each piece.

6. And, finally, with the last color of paper, fold and cut until you have sixteenths. Label and initial.

Make sure to have each student store their initialed pieces in a separate container. You don't want to have to sort these all out at some point. That's the purpose of the initials.

Origami Napping House

(Chapter 13 – Connecting Math With Literature)

1. Give each student an 8 ½" x 11" piece of white computer paper.

2. Fold the paper in half to get a long rectangle. This is known as a "hot dog" fold.

3. Open the paper and fold it in half to make a fat rectangle, or a "hamburger fold."

4. Fold each side of the hamburger fold in to meet the center line you made with the hot dog fold. Crease well.

5. Open the fold on each side and push down the top of the upper corners to make a triangle that lines up with the left and right side crease.

6. Open each side and push the triangle flat. Crease.

7. You'll have a shape which looks a bit like a house with two doors that will open.

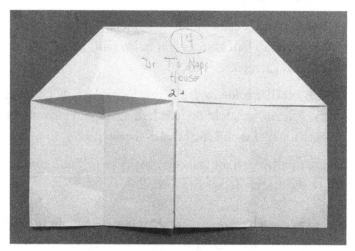

The Napping House with doors closed

The Napping House with doors open

Happy Hundred Chicken Noodle Soup
(Chapter 16 – The Hundredth Day of School)

> A carton of low sodium chicken broth
> An equal amount of water
> Spaghetti noodles broken into one-inch pieces
> Ditalini noodles (little round noodles that look like zeros)

Bring the broth and the water to a boil.

Add both types of noodles and cook until the ditalini softens.

Serve in tiny cups until it's all gone.

Paper book for playing Circles and Stars
(Chapter 17 – Math Buddies)

1. Give each student an 8 ½ X 11 inch piece of white computer paper
2. Fold the paper in half to get a long rectangle. This is known as a "hot dog" fold.
3. Then open the paper and fold it in half to make a fat rectangle, or a "hamburger fold."
4. Keep the hamburger fold in place and fold from the bottom, taking the bottom flap of the paper on one side up to meet the top and creasing at the midpoint.
5. Turn the paper over and take the second flap up and fold when it meets the top of this side of the paper, just as you did on the other side.

6. Hold onto the paper where that original hamburger fold in the middle of the sheet is. Let the side flaps hang down. Your hand will be holding the center fold at the center point of the original hot dog fold.

7. Carefully tear just halfway down on the hot dog fold. You can see where it meets the other folds so stop right there.

8. Now hold the paper on the hamburger fold line, one hand on each side of the tear. Bring the paper sides down to meet and make a four section structure.

9. Wrap all the folded sections together to make a 3" x 4 ½" book shape with four pages.

Fold together to make a book shape.

Race to One Hundred Calculator game

(Chapter 20 – Parent/Teacher Relations)

Each player has a calculator. At the signal "Go," players +1 on the calculator. That is, 1+1+1+1... The winner is the person who gets to 100 first. A variation is, on their turn, players roll either one or two dice, add that number on the calculator but also keep a running record on paper. Again, the winner is the first player to reach 100.

Green Eggs and Ham

(Chapter 21 – Theodore Seuss Geisel and Shel Silverstein)

Ingredients:

> A few chunks of ham, finely diced
> Cooking oil, about 1 tablespoon
> One egg for each person
> Some milk, about one teaspoon/egg
> Salt and pepper
> Green food coloring

Directions: Get the oil hot in a frying pan and sauté the ham just for a few minutes. Lower the heat. Crack the eggs into a bowl and whip lightly with a fork or whisk. Add milk, salt and pepper and enough food coloring to get an appetizing shade of green and stir together. Pour the eggs into the pan and mix with the ham. Cook until eggs are set.

ACKNOWLEDGEMENTS

First of all, a great deal of the credit for the fact this book ever saw the light of day goes to my "midwives." These are the women in my Writer's Club - Jean Berg, Claire Poulson, Donna Hatfield, and Marilin Campbell. Over a period of several years, we have all met and shared our writings and they have encouraged me in my efforts to produce this story about my life as a teacher. Many thanks to you, ladies.

I also want to thank the teachers and the administrator who sent me anecdotes about their own adventures as educators – Gene Bratek, Peggy Leftakis, Mardi McMakin, Joanne McCarthy, Amy Diamond, Marsha Ranieri and my sister-in-law, Judy. Thank you, Sarah Henry, for your generous sharing of useful information on math manipulatives.

Thanks to my son Patrick, my Internet sleuth and technology consultant.

And thanks to the following colleagues, friends, and family members who contributed to my development as a teacher and who helped me pull this book together – Michael Thrailkill, Patrick Thrailkill, Roger Thrailkill, Rita Tucker, Pat Summers, Carol Noonan, Mary McCown, George Winston, Michelle Kay Doeden, Donna Yoncovig, Kim Smith, Christine Williams, Nicholas Kontaridis, Karel Lucander, Dorothy Thrailkill, Kristin Retort, Pam Brunschwyler, Raymond Aldridge, Leanna Isaacson, Charlotte Barolet, James Kaiser, Carol Reid, and Angela Baucom.

And, of course, thank you to every student, thousands of you, who crossed my path and enriched my life.

CPSIA information can be obtained
at www.ICGtesting.com
Printed in the USA
LVHW031930180221
679455LV00016B/558

9 781480 899544